KV-575-832

Folklore in Use
Applications in the Real World

Aims and Scope

Folklore in Use: Applications in the Real World offers a forum for the discussion of folklore theory and practice outside traditional academic settings. It is devoted to the publication of original research, brief review articles, short communications, commentary, opinion and book and film reviews on all aspects of "folklore-in-use" in the community at large. This journal encourages discourse on the challenges — personal, professional and political — of applying folklore concepts and methods, not only to cultural conservation, but also to social process and change. It will examine the role of folklorists in such areas as: public presentations of traditional culture, community involvement and advocacy, health care, organizational management, politics, the media, the legal system and education. **Folklore in Use** is aimed not only at folklorists, however, but all practitioners active in workplaces and communities — in museums, schools and libraries, in factories and offices, in town halls and union halls, in public and private sectors — grappling with the role, image and use of traditional culture in the world at large.

Editor

David Shuldiner

Instructions for Authors

As the 'Aims and Scope' statement implies, it is the intention of this journal to reach not only across disciplines, but beyond them as well, so that practitioners dealing with the interface of traditional culture and the community at large, but without formal training in folklore methods and concepts, may still participate in the ongoing discussions about 'folklore-in-use' presented in the journal. It is in this spirit that the following guidelines for submissions are offered:

1. Submissions should be sent to David Shuldiner, Editor, *Folklore in Use*, 155 Linnmoore Street, Hartford CT 06114, USA. Please submit two copies typed double-spaced on one side of standard 8.5" x 11" or A4 paper. If at all possible, include a DOS-compatible disk (either 3.5" or 5.25"), preferably in WordPerfect, Wordstar or ASCII format. Detailed guidelines for preparing files to facilitate typesetting are available from the publishers.

2. You may submit a theoretical article, a critique of other writings on 'folklore-in-use', a 'position paper' on a particular issue (to which readers may respond in subsequent issues), or a 'report from the field' (factory, office, community, etc.). Review articles (books and films) as well as critiques of public folklore presentations (exhibits, festivals and other projects, programs, displays or events) are also encouraged. Feel free to review related items in a single article.

3. Please write as clearly as possible, avoiding all unnecessary jargon — your audience will include non-specialists. Footnotes are discouraged; endnotes are acceptable but please keep them to a minimum. Citations may be made in parentheses in the body of an article, i.e. (Smith 1990). References may be cited at the end of an article; refer to recent issues of the *Journal of American Folklore* for bibliographical models.

4. Articles will generally be submitted to readers for peer review. Suggestions for revisions may be made; the Editor, however, will assume responsibility for final copy.

5. Contributors will ordinarily be asked to grant copyright to the publishers; however, special arrangements can be made, especially for contributors working for public agencies.

Subscription Information

Folklore in Use is published twice annually. Subscription rates for Volume 2 are £20.00 UK institutions, £10.00 UK individuals. Send payments to Hisarlik Press, 4 Catisfield Road, Enfield Lock, Middlesex EN3 6BD, UK, or credit card details to Vine House Distribution, Waldenbury, North Common, Chailey, East Sussex, BN8 4DR, UK.

Editorial correspondences should be addressed to David Shuldiner at the above address. Business correspondence should be addressed to: Hisarlik Press, 4 Catisfield Road, Enfield Lock, Middlesex EN3 6BD, UK. Tel. +44 992 700 898; fax +44 81 292 6118; e-mail *fiu@hisarlik.demon.co.uk*

Folklore in Use 2, 1–11 (1994)

Preface

The Marketing of Tradition

Teri Brewer

THE CONFERENCE

The papers which make up this special issue of *Folklore in Use* originate from a (British) Folklore Society conference held at the University of Glamorgan in Wales in June 1994. The subject we met to explore was "The Marketing of Tradition". It's a topic on the minds of many of us working in fields touching on matters of folklore, heritage, tradition and cultural preservation. So it seemed a useful talking point for the second in a series of small conferences meant to take stock and consider the future for folklore studies and for folkloristics (i.e. the methodological and theoretical underpinnings) in the British Isles. We encouraged international participation from people who had either an interest in the folklore of the British Isles, or who were working on problems and experiences relevant to our concerns. We were pleased to see not only a strong representation of Canadian and American folklorists join us, but also to welcome interest from people in fields outside folklore studies or ethnology and from beyond academia.

For most readers of these papers, whether students, academics, museum curators, public folklorists, community programs specialists, development officers, tourism advisors or employees in new sectors of the burgeoning Heritage industry, the issues and questions raised in this collection will, we hope, be stimulating. They need to be. The problems identified are ethically complex, critical and widespread. The literature on the topic at present is diffuse, if fascinating. (See the appended brief introductory bibliography for some ideas about further reading).

The theme of the first conference, held in 1993, was "British Folklore Studies: Past, Present and Prospects." The past was usefully gleaned there (a powerful metaphor developed by keynote speaker Bill Nicolaisen), but people seemed uncertain about how to discuss visions of alternative futures, being uncertain about present possibilities. Questions and issues that recurred there seemed to focus on participants' relationships with the perceived commodification of tradition or heritage.

How do we think about the juxtaposition of heritage with industry? What role, if any, do specialists in folklore want to play in increasingly commercial markets for traditional knowledge? In what ways may we be driven by the contemporary economic imperatives which now frequently impel the commercial exploitation of traditionalia, or the institutional marketability of our interests? A decision was made to base the 1994 conference on the theme: The Marketing of Tradition.

This issue of *Folklore in Use* includes all but three of the 1994 papers. Sadly, because of deadlines and prior commitments, we were not able to print Steve Siporin's paper, Paul Smith's paper or the paper by Sandy Hobbs and David Cornwell. Hobb's and Cornwell's piece, "Sawney Bean, the Scottish Cannibal" explores a local legend which has migrated from Galloway to South Ayrshire and in the process become a draw for tourists. Siporin's study, "Jackalopes, Fur Bearing Trout and Watermelons on Skids: The Traditional Marketing of Tradition," reflects on tall tales, and regional boosterism in the United States, the real antecedent of today's more organized and commercial regional representation, and one which runs in parallel to it still. He concentrates on an exploration of fabulous postcard images, the nature of which are indicated in the title. Paul Smith mapped out some new directions in his paper "A Theoretical Framework for the Study of Marketing Tradition."

All three of these papers reported work in progress, and the subjects are noted here so that readers who are interested can watch for later publication. We chose to include an updated version of one of the 1993 papers (Harvey) because it seemed to anticipate some of the themes of the 1994 conference, and fit well with the rest of the papers presented here.

The order of articles in this issue reflects what seeemed logical groupings, beginning with some genre and transmission issues raised in papers by Petford, Niles and Harvey, we go on to a series of case studies of regional examples and praxis. The collection ends with a trilogy of papers on some of the more exotic manifestations of the ancient and rather sophisticated Celtic Heritage industry.

- Josey Petford opened the conference by considering a shift in the expectations of Heritage industry audiences. She suggests that tomorrow's consumer, increasingly influenced by new technologies, will expect and be won over by experiences which are actively involving. This ironically brings a vision of an audience that no longer wants to be informed about tradition (the consequence of literacy) but to play at being part of it.

- Clodagh Harvey's paper suggests some of the ground to be covered. The "storytelling revival" is no new phenomenon, being well advanced in North America for instance, but has only recently developed real momentum in the British Isles. She explores the development of the revival in Northern Ireland and in the Republic of Ireland, setting it in the context of her previous work on pre-revival storytelling traditions.

- The marketing of tradition, as John Niles points out in his discussion of three commercial documentary film-makers' work, seems like a paradoxical activity, but is actually one which has plenty of precedent. He considers folk-documentary as a marketed form.

- Gwendolyn Leick surveys some presentations of a pre-Arabic past in several parts of the Middle East, and considers the role that such presentations play for internal and external consumers.

- Viv Loveday examines the systemic conflict created by the development of historical expertise on the part of re-enactors working in the Heritage industry. They may increasingly cross swords with a potentially threatened academic establishment, felt to be unexpectedly losing control over the interpretation of the past.

- John Sheets and Gerald Thomas each focus on particular and powerful personalities on whose behalfs they have almost inadvertently become advocates. Sheets and Thomas have played a role in re-presentation of someone else's life and work to an audience beyond the community of origin as well as influencing the community memory and view of those individuals.

- Patricia Atkinson Wells, on the other hand, reports on the problems that folk artists and performers may encounter in marketing themselves, and discusses her experience in organizing workshops meant to help them cope with the experience. Her paper also resonates with Gerald Thomas' description of his experience helping to manage Emile Benoit's musical career.

- Pauline Young and Ann Berriman approach the subject of marketed tradition from dissimilar but linked perspectives. Young's work on Fay Weldon is a case study in the astute use of traditional motifs and themes in novels which have achieved both critical acclaim and commercial success. Berriman discusses her experience in writing and producing plays on local heritage for staging at historical sites in Australia.

- Juliette Wood's paper is a study of a particular corner of Arthuriana—the marketed images and object, comics, novels, china, tarot cards, some sold as curios to pilgrims at sites associated with Arthurian legend, some mass-produced for a world-wide market, some fairly esoteric materials for those with specialist historical or spiritual interests.

• Leslie Jones glances, tongue in cheek, at the results of a particular market niche in cosmopolitan heritage publishing—a recent florescence of innovative and syncretic do-it-yourself manuals for the aspiring postmodern druidic shaman, and considers the relationship of the same to a range of fascinating precedents.

• Marion Bowman is pan-Celtic rather than post-Celtic in her discussion of the conjunction of New Age spirituality with neo-Celtic marketing practices.

BETWEEN AND BEYOND THE PAPERS

The relationship of folklore to tradition is usually only considered in carefully delimited arenas. These papers are a good example of that tendency. Each is based on description and reflection and the analyses reflect some degree of shared assumption about the historical and contemporary contexts discussed. When reading these papers it is useful to reflect on the relationship to macro-social processes. Regional, national and international markets embody informal synchronic or diachronic micro-social processes, as well as being spheres of commerce. Consider the conversion of social processes to products that is illustrated in many of these papers. As became clear during the conference, it is increasingly necessary for us, as observers and consultants, to have some theoretical models to try to understand or evaluate such connections. These essays are still concerned primarily with the action within fairly small arenas, but there is something more developing interstitially, I think, and I will make some tentative comments about the emic model which seems to arise from the conjunction of the papers.

While it is impossible to capture the whole flavor of a lively forum between these pages or even to sample all of the voices in discussion, many of the papers have been revised to reflect the debates provoked in live presentation as well as in response to the comments of referees. This should further the sense of articulation between papers. Each presenter has chosen to discuss specific materials or situations well known to them through fieldwork and research. It remains for me to try to draw out some of the common themes and preoccupations, and to suggest what some of the underlying problems and necessary questions might be.

I will begin by talking about the primary audience at this conference, because a perception of audience so influences the presentations we make. Not everyone who participated in this conference was a folklorist, but all shared a common interest in aspects of folklore or in tradition. But the audience for the papers was perceived as being primarily folklorists by those giving papers, and therefore a certain degree of common background and preoccupation was assumed. How safe is this? The Folklore Society in Britain has the distinctive characteristic of being eclectic and particularly diverse in membership. This is a consequence of a number of historical factors which need not be gone into here, but it is worth pointing out that the society is *not* primarily a professional association for academics and public sector folklorists. In this it is at least unusual amongst scholarly societies. People from many occupations and backgrounds have shared a common interest in the processes of transmission of custom, in exploring the origins of things too often taken for granted, in preserving or creating forms of knowledge which can at first glance seem arcane, in understanding the patterns and histories of everyday culture and the social groupings that create and transmit them. Their membership in the Folklore Society brings them together, but the focus of their interests is often quite sharp and practical, antiquarian or collectorial, rather than theoretically or paradigmatically based.

When we focus individually on what may seem passionate, private and possibly esoteric interests, we can lose any sense of how, why and for whom folklore or tradition is publicly framed, consumed or purveyed. When folklore or traditional behaviors become part of the stock-in-trade for tourism and Heritage industries, whether as *processes* (represented in the re-enactments discussed by Loveday or Petford, the dramatizations described by Berriman, the self-improvement projects discussed by Bowman or Jones, the work analyzed by Wells) or as *products* (films such as those chosen by Niles, postcards, stories and regional kitsch as documented by Siporin, Hobbs and Cornwell and Wood, or political and cultural appropriations of the kind examined by Leick) change in attitudes to folklore over time inevitably effects a kind of contextual shift of scale which is easily overlooked. A sense of this shift is vital for everyone with interests in folklore because it will affect them directly sooner or later.

There is nothing either esoteric or exotic about folklore in small-scale context, that is, material aimed at an audience reasonably intimate with the producers. It is often so deeply imbedded in the lives and minds of a community that little discussion is considered necessary. But in some quarters it is still common to assume that 'folklore' is a euphemism for moribund culture or that at best it constituted a set of false beliefs associated with primitive mentalities (fortunately) now on the wane in

the march of civilization and that traditionality is an unfortunate
condition which should soon pass.

> Traditional peoples had only a limited perception of time and space.
> The time with which they were familiar was the present, and their
> minds reached back only to their childhood. Of the vast span of time
> that had gone before they had heard only vague rumors, and these
> they conflated with stories of creation, of giants and of mythical
> heroes. (Pounds 1994:407)

Most readers of *Folklore in Use* would probably agree to a rather
different perspective on folklore, seeing it as the manifestation of
processes of communication and transmission associated with quite often
informal and flexible group identities (see Bowman's discussion of
'elective affinities'), which may be based on occupation, ethnicity, gender,
age, or other unifying factors. As such we usually agree that it is as likely
to be found in contemporary city life as in isolated rural communities
and that it is as common amongst cyberpunks and bureaucrats as
amongst peasants and lumberjacks.

But what about tradition? Isn't there a tendency to see tradition as a
victim of modernity? Don't we often seem to assume that traditional
crafts, customs, sayings and music are disappearing under the advance
of literacy, standardization, franchising, the recording studio, industrialization and postmodern reflexive irony?

Despite the broader perspective on folklore that we may share, the net
is not cast so widely here. Why not? The papers here are concerned with
matters of *marketable* tradition—that is, what some agents of change in
several societies discussed perceive as the *unique* and *externally presentable*
cultural heritage of those societies, the acceptable face of the past in
many cases, and those aspects of it which are not too private to share
with outsiders. In other words, how they can interestingly represent and
package their own cultural traditions as a valued and valuable commodity for certain prescribed sorts of internal consumption as well as for
tourists from abroad?

Why would anybody want to do that? Is it a form of diplomacy? Is it
to encourage immigration? Why the sudden increase of concern about
what the neighbors think in the late twentieth century?

ECONOMIC, POLITICAL AND DEMOGRAPHIC FACTORS

The answer to these questions lies beyond the levels on which we usually
analyze our interests. These marketings are driven by the pragmatics of
demography, economy and politics which are never divorced from the

intimate world of folklore and tradition, but are too rarely explored. The marketing of tradition, a concept which seems paradoxical and perhaps amusing on first glance, is a very serious business indeed. Highlighting and retailing a sense of shared tradition is often successful when used by individuals and political factions (either within or outside the focal community) to gain personal or collective influence, to advance policies, improve or undermine social cohesion for motives which may be either altruistic or selfish.

Appeals to a sense of communal heritage or traditionality touch powerful emotions because they go to the heart of individual, family, community and sometimes national or regional identities. Behaviors, products, places, stories and beliefs characterized as traditional can achieve a transcendence as they metamorphose from the familiar and the comfortable and become charged and potentially multivalent symbols. Such symbols, significantly, may be interpreted differently depending on whether one is part of the tradition or not.

SOME ECONOMIC CONSIDERATIONS

The economic drive to market tradition is often based on the need to make an income for people in a region where rapid economic change has de-stabilized or destroyed alternative job markets. Where populations are high or the economy is weak and mobility is low, the development of tourism is often a major or primary industry. This is a pragmatic form of conjuring for those charged with getting quick solutions for serious problems. There is however another motivation for economic development of traditional materials which is traced in the last three papers in the collection. The development of social and spiritual counter-cultures is often accompanied by a necessary commitment to creating alternative economies. This allows participants to live more fully within their created world as well as to fulfil the needs of special markets created by alternity. In the case of the New Age movements this creates demands for traditional knowledge transmitted in book form or a variety of material goods and services such as those discussed by Jones, Bowman and Wood.

In a world where an increasing number of goods and services are standardized and internationally distributed by large corporations the world can seem a less varied place for the tourist who wants to see something different from home. The encapsulation of travellers as package(d) tourists, who want to see and to be seen to have seen, but who don't want sights to be threatening or alarming or requiring great effort to comprehend, drive us to package our cultures for easy and palatable and fast consumption. Our need for some privacy from excessive tourist interest may reinforce the tendency. This is a different audience, or market, from the one described by Petford, and it is important to note that there are different audiences for the same traditions.

If we can't be too strange, too threatening or too familiar, and we have to be explicable, how better to achieve that end than to use the infinitely elastic, malleable and often well-sourced past, and to focus on tradition and unique heritage as *the* marketable commodity for the twenty-first century? Observations of this solution have not been infrequent recently. The bittersweet tone of social commentary has seized particularly on the dangers of planning a future based on freezing and re-enacting the past in so self-conscious a way. This is widely seen as a vital contemporary dilemma, discussed even in fiction such as Joanne Greenberg's eerie view of the man from SCELPP (the Social, Cultural and Ethnic Life Placement Program) in her satirical novel *Simple Gifts* (Greenberg 1987).

THE DEMOGRAPHIC

Demographers and geographers map shifts in population and shifts in the use of space. Usually we think of this as being about patterns of residence—how human communities and their relationship to the landscape change over time. Cultural geographers can go further and map other kinds of space utilization and suggest possible consequences for social interaction. In his paper on Colonsay, John Sheets has suggested several ways that demographic change impinges on tradition, and creates new axes of interest. He shows the importance of noting whether populations increase or decrease in particular places and why— whether they live in dispersed rural settlements, nucleated villages, towns or urban sprawl.

Folklore is an intimate synchronic practice, but not one necessarily requiring geographical intimacy. It is not a closed system, though it may be highly coded and self referential. It is often a matter of group survival and there is often little or no direct concern with having an influence external to the group. It can be transmitted through time, but seldom remains static in transmission.

When it becomes *popular culture* it moves beyond the network of origin through the deliberate agency of individuals who may not themselves be part of the originating group. As part of popular culture, broader referents of knowledge or behavior are interpretable in at least a limited way, whether or not they are actively used by individuals in the larger society. (This is where much adaptation of folklore and traditional materials for advertizing purposes comes in—it is evocative and perhaps attractive because of the recognition that there is more than meets the eye here). In this larger audience, where performer and audience may not be known to one another and where material may be use in contexts other than the elective affinity group for which the behavior was initially directly relevant and interpretable, origins will probably not be well understood. But is it necessary for them to be? Resonances rather than specific meanings become most important.

With transformation to *"cultural heritage"* intent is maximized as a motivation. The agenda is increasingly impersonal and political. Information or behavior is used as a tool to extenuate the impact of agendas which may have little to do with the material promoted. Informal transmission is less important than adoption by powerbrokers when agendas of status and power in large social arenas are being negotiated. It is here where commodification really begins to develop. Attempts to control social processes have met with limited success. Only the promised technologies of virtual reality give promise of satisfactory control over apparently present events.

THE POLITICAL

Folkloristics is not just about ways of approaching the description of tradition or the evolution of tradition. Rather it should give us ways to approach an understanding of the *uses* of tradition, and therefore a more explicit take on cultural politics. In these papers attention is drawn to the juncture of folklore and popular culture, where private signs become familiar referents to people from outside the original knowing network. Being a beach-town Californian, I know some surfer slang, and I am aware of some of the other aspects of the folk culture of surfers, but I am not and never was a member of that group and I wouldn't ordinarily *use* their special group vocabulary, styles, signals or rituals. But I know that their small folk culture has now influenced international popular culture, and as an in-group language, surfer dress and style have all become fashionable amongst kids far from any surfing beaches. A lot of this shift from folk culture and local tradition has to do with marketing. Products are often sold by evoking the fragrance of exotic lifestyle and image; old Beach Boy's songs and images of woodies (the nickname for cars popular with surfers in my childhood) sell products which have nothing to do with surfers, or California, Hawaii, Australia or other locations pictured, but rather to do with dreams of freedom and romantic otherness. They are also used by association to sell California itself as a tourist location, disorienting to natives, who know the surfers as only a small part of their world.

One of my favorite examples of an interesting commercial and cultural marketing dyslexia about California beach culture is an ad for a liqueur often shown on British television in recent years. A couple walk along a sunset sea, coconut palms in the background, steel drums playing a Caribbean melody. The voice-over is done by a man with a deep and resonant Jamaican accent. He just says: "Malibu—a taste of paradise". What more is there to say? More than you might think if you are not a local.

The paradise depicted bears no relation to Malibu the place—a stretch of coast and a town north-west of Los Angeles in California. The real Malibu is a place of rugged oak- and cactus-studded mountains and canyons which fall abruptly to the chilly Pacific Ocean. The coast is mostly rather rocky, neither gentle nor tropical, and the tourists are more inclined to movie star spotting than to rum drinking and steel bands. The name Malibu is an anglicized version of an older Chumash Indian name for this stretch of coast, but the outsider's perceptual needs are more important in marketing the drink than any truth about the name or the place.

ACKNOWLEDGEMENTS

I would like to thank Dr Jacqueline Simpson, president of the Folklore Society, and Dr Frances Mannsåker, head of the School of Humanities and Social Sciences at the University of Glamorgan, for the support given to this conference. I would also like to thank Mrs Mary Earl, the School Administrator, for her incomparable logistical assistance and wise counsel. Elizabeth Coviello did much of the work behind the scenes and was the *éminence grise* of record keeping. Patricia Wells found herself unexpectedly part of the organizing team and played a vital last minute role with her usual grace, calm and wit. Gwendolyn Leick and Josey Petford organized conference hospitality and an extraordinary pre-conference trip most memorably. Thanks are also due to Viv Loveday and Pauline Young, as well as to all the participants, both presenters and audience. They made this an exceptional conference. It is unusual to thank other Universities, but I think it in order to thank the faculty and students of the Folklore Department at Memorial University of New-foundland in Canada, and the staff and students of the MA program in Welsh Ethnology (Department of Welsh) at the University of Wales in Cardiff for their stalwart support and extraordinary turnout.

SOME SUGGESTIONS FOR FURTHER READING

Baron, Robert and N. Spitzer. 1992. *Public Folklore.* Washington: Smithsonian Institution Press.

Buck, Elizabeth. 1993. *Paradise Remade: The Politics of Culture and History in Hawai'i.* Philadelphia: Temple University Press.

Cantwell, Robert. 1993. *Ethnomimesis: Folklife and the Representation of Culture.* Chapel Hill: University of North Carolina Press.

Connerton, Paul. 1989. *How Societies Remember.* Cambridge: Cambridge University Press.

Dilley, Roy. 1991. Contesting Markets. *Anthropology Today* 7:4:14–18.

Evans, John. 1994. *How Real is My Valley? Postmodernism and the South Wales Valleys.* Pontypridd: Underground Press.

Greenberg, Joanne. 1986. *Simple Gifts.* New York: Henry Holt & Co.

Hewison, Robert. 1987. *The Heritage Industry: Britain in a Climate of Decline.* London: Methuen.

Hobsbawm, Eric and T. Ranger. 1983. *The Invention of Tradition.* Cambridge: Cambridge University Press.

Hufford, Mary Ann. 1994. *Conserving Culture: A New Discourse on Heritage.* Urbana: University of Illinois Press.

Jenkins, Geraint. 1992. *Getting Yesterday Right: Interpreting the Heritage of Wales.* Cardiff: University of Wales Press.

Loomis, Ormond. 1983. *Cultural Conservation: The Protection of Cultural Heritage in the United States.* Washington DC: Library of Congress.

Ritzer, George. 1993. *The McDonaldization of Society.* London: Pine Forge Press.

Shils, Edward. 1977. *Tradition.* Chicago: University of Chicago Press.

Tonkin, Elizabeth, et al. 1989. *History and Ethnicity.* London: Routledge.

Trosset, Carol. 1994. *Welshness Performed.* Tucson: University of Arizona Press.

Whisnant, David. 1983. *All That is Native and Fine: The Politics of Culture in an American Region.* Chapel Hill: University of North Carolina Press.

Williams, Raymond. 1976. *Keywords.* London: Fontana.

Folklore in Use 2, 13–23 (1994)

Seeing Is Believing—The Role of Living History In Marketing Local Heritage

Josey Petford

Re-enactment and Living History displays are becoming increasingly popular as ways of attracting tourists to "Heritage sites." For some locations this has involved the development of new attractions specifically built to house first-person interpretation, an effort to construct time pockets where traditional skills can be re-enacted with traditional implements and visitors treated to the sounds and smells of times past. Others, in particular such bodies as English Heritage, perhaps lacking the capital or a willingness to speculate with scarce resources in what could be a passing fashion in Heritage marketing, encourage outsiders, often amateur outsiders, to use their facilities and enhance their public attractions. But whatever the format, there is hardly a Heritage site in Britain that does not use Living History of some description to entice the public through the gates. What is it about pike-wielding soldiers and costumed retainers that is so irresistible to both public and business alike? What do they offer that even the best static display cannot? Explanations vary, for some the advantages of living history lie in its ability to illustrate social relationships, a dimension of history that is very difficult to put over effectively in static displays; for others it offers the public live action, something they are accustomed to getting in a televisual age.

This paper is an attempt to raise some of the issues surrounding the use of living history and, bearing in mind the televisual sophistication of today's audiences, its relationship to interactive multimedia technology and the utilization and impact of both within the heritage industry. They are issues which have been widely discussed before but not, as far as I am aware, together. It will not offer any answers, not simply because I sincerely believe that there are no easy ones, but also because this paper is only part of a larger and much more comprehensive piece of work currently being written.

Today, in the age of PCs and lap tops, technology increasingly invades our lives and as it does so, it not only changes many of our traditional methods of working but is also starting to influence the way we see and relate to the world. Computer conferencing, and Internet systems could revolutionize the way we communicate. Distance and context are all relative when it is possible to check the current state of the surf in Florida or the coffee machine at Cambridge simply by typing in the correct address on Internet. Equally revolutionary, working from home no longer involves transporting large quantities of paperwork on the train, indeed it may mean not leaving home at all but just hooking up my PC to a modem and having a chat with head office that could well be a continent away. Home working and computer cottaging is being hailed as the beginning of a reversal of the urbanization which, in its time, revolutionized working practice and social structures during industrialization.

A common sight today, at least so we are lead to believe by television advertising, is the child, Gameboy grasped in hand, fighting the controls, attention totally concentrated on the machine while the rest of the world passes by. In fact computer games are fast becoming a major challenge to television in the competition for children's and adult's time and money. Phillips have recently answered the challenge by releasing CDI, which, according to a Phillips advertisement means that—"Television is no longer just something you watch, its something you do." (Phillips advertising campaign, broadcast UK 1994) and this marketing strategy sheds some light on the essence of the battle currently being waged by the heritage industry.

Interactivity is the buzz word of the 1990s and the battle lines have been drawn in the war to woo the consumer with claims of total participation and experience. No longer does leisure have to consist of something that done to us, now we have the chance to be the center of any action taking place. This can take the form of choosing the ultimate football team for a computer simulation of the World Cup, entry to a theme park where characters from stage, screen and legend can hold your hand, or a visit to a historical site complete with living, breathing time travelers. We are told by those in the know that only the complete experience suits the consumer in this age of interactivity and there is promise of more to come. It is now possible to look around a museum without ever leaving your living room, and it is suggested that in a few years it should be possible to visit that same museum, walk around the exhibits, pick up and handle the artifacts, converse with experts and maybe even start a romantic liaison without ever moving from the comfort of your arm chair and virtual reality suit. The entertainment industry, as much a victim of its own publicity as the public it seeks to convince, is already harnessing these, as yet embryonic, technologies. By offering consumers 'movie rides', four minutes of wraparound sound and vision complemented by hydraulic seating platforms which create the illusion of participation in the movie action, they also create an illusion of an easy technological sophistication, which in reality has only been purchased through exorbitant expenditure amounting millions in time and money.

Having acknowledged that the leisure industry is aiming for inter-activity as a priority strategy for enticing new consumers I want to explore the possible results of this move, the differences between and interconnectedness of two, superficially quite different, forms of interactivity, multi-media and living history, and look into the possible futures of both, how they can exist in complement or how technology could result in the partial superseding of humans by computer simulation.

Primarily however I would like to make a brief diversion into the roots of these two media of transmission. Where exactly do Multimedia and Living history come from?

The original multi-media experiences, in the days before computers, used conventional media like slides, music, live action and film such as that used by L. Frank Baum to present one of his many versions of the Oz stories. Later versions of multimedia, aimed primarily at a student audience, used TV, video, radio, text, slides and student/teacher interactions. This system showed the advantages of multimedia teaching, that learning and retention of information are greatly enhanced when written, aural, visual and experiential forms of presentation are utilized, but also highlighted the cumbersome nature of the, then current, technology.

Back in the 1960s computers took up whole rooms and demanded an experts knowledge to perform the simplest of tasks. The idea of computers in schools, let alone in museums or on street corners was an impossible and future dream. And yet with the progress in computer technology in the 1980s, multimedia and the interactive systems which utilize that technology, are now starting to appear in schools in the form of multimedia encyclopedias and in the leisure industry, as replacements for traditional audio-visual displays (Martlew, 1990). The production of this technology has, to a large extent been through packages for use in military and more commercial settings. Military exercises are now conducted both through computer simulation and on the ground, where software has been designed to confound the 'real' and the 'hyper-real', the target which really drives along a real road and that which does so simply on the simulator. It is possible to wander through a shop which exists only in virtual space inside a computer, or get double glazing advice from a computer generated expert, before proceeding to purchase the raw materials.

In effect, what multimedia offers is the chance for both children and adults to learn at their own speed through exploring a computer generated environment which includes full or half page video, animation, graphics, sound effects, music, and text. This self guided form of learning removes the teacher from the central role of controller of information and places them in the more peripheral role of facilitator, the person who guides the learner's access to knowledge, or, in the case of commercial settings, the firm which provides the technology.

Schools have also been some of the first to exploit another type of interactive learning primarily found in the Heritage industry and this growing medium of transmission raises some interesting points that can be related back to multimedia. But first it is important to explore exactly what is meant by living history.

There are many faces to living history, for example in Britain the New Model Army Society, a group of amateurs who reenact English Civil War battles, has a small, but growing contingent of Living History buffs, who set up and live in "authentic camps" at their battles. The public is then invited to look around the camps, with supervision of course, and experience the living conditions of the average Civil War soldier. This is one aspect of living history, one which is done primarily for love of an era and a desire to empathize with the period re-enacted. At the conference where this paper was first presented there was an opportunity to visit a local heritage site, Llancaiach Fawr, another form of living history exhibit which is aimed at a commercial market and is staffed by professional interpreters. This site utilizes first person interpretation, and the company which was employed to set up the interpretation, Past Pleasures, is run by Mark Wallace who learnt his trade at Plimoth Plantation in New England, the progenitor of all modern living history sites. But what can living history offer that traditional media cannot? The answer lies in the social dimensions of culture.

A community's history, whether carried by the oral or written word, through folklore or in books, acts as centralizing force around which identities, communal or personal, are formed. A miner is a miner not just because he works in a mine but because he belongs to a mining community which has formed over time based around a commonalty of lifestyle and expectations. Over many years this dimension of communities has provided museums with a major hurdle when trying to communicate to visitors the complexity of the cultures from which their artifacts are drawn. A static display, behind glass cases with little labels to give information cannot even start to explain the social dimensions of a culture. The folklife museums of the late nineteenth and early twentieth centuries attempted to confront this problem but what they offered were only sanitized performances of isolated traditional crafts. In other cases displays were limited to rescued relocated buildings which, although providing a useful resource in themselves, again fail to communicate the social base of communities.

The idea of introducing people in costume onto the sites and into the buildings really took off in the United States in 1932 with the opening of Colonial Williamsburg staffed by costumed hostesses to act as guides, but without attempting to adopt the roles of the original inhabitants. 1947 saw the opening of Plimoth Plantation in New England, a specially constructed village to illustrate the lives of the first settlers, but again the costumed staff simply acted as guides and told visitors about the problems, social structure and everyday lives of the plantation residents. Towards the end of the 1970s however a peculiar phenomenon started to arise. Instead of communicating in the third person and acting as guides, the staff started to refer to the activities on the site in the first person using terms such as 'we do' rather than 'they did'. This saw the birth of first-person interpretation, a policy which was officially adopted by Plimoth Plantation in 1978.

Since then this form of interpretation has spread like wildfire. Its obvious theatrical advantages over third person interpretation giving it a pulling power that historical sites, faced with increasing competition and a finite number of visitors, could not ignore. In Britain today it is difficult to find a heritage site brochure that does not carry as part of its forthcoming attractions some element of living history either by staff who work for the site itself or by visiting amateur or professional groups.

Schools have been quick to exploit this as a teaching resource and many use living history sites for introductory explorations into a new period. Allowing children to spend a day in a Victorian classroom can give a very different insight than any amount of book learning could. Ten-year-old girls, accustomed to wearing jeans and riding BMX bikes can start to understand the limitations a long skirt and hat put on their behavior, something they could never hope to learn from a book. And a cold, dark classroom with chalk and a slate to write with, and a teacher demanding the children recite the lesson or sit in absolute silence is a far cry from sitting in a centrally heated one with posters on the walls whilst discussing the differences.

It's not really hard to see what both these forms of learning and entertainment have in common. Both living history and multimedia potentially offer a high level of interactivity which add both to their entertainment level and to their ability to teach. What better way of teaching can there be but to slip in important facts while people are looking the other way enjoying themselves. But can any media claim to be educational as well as entertaining. Surely the temptation is there in a competitive market, to exploit the more exciting elements of history at the cost of the more mundane. For example Llancaiach Fawr markets itself primarily as the house where Charles I lunched on his way from Brecon to Abergavenny. For those unacquainted with the geography of the South Wales region, this would mean a detour of some forty miles on horse back through the Welsh valleys only to double back to Raglan Castle the following day. In reality it is highly likely that the King actually visited another Prichard in Grosmont, almost directly in his line of march but this probability is ignored in order to exploit the more commercially viable 'King's Visit'. The fact that Prichard would be turning in his grave at being accused, as a staunch Parliamentarian and Baptist, of entertaining the King and being a turn coat is also ignored, as are the possibilities of using Llancaiach Fawr as a illustration of how religious and political beliefs often went hand in hand in the seventeenth century. Museums, having to compete in the open market, cannot afford to let reality get in the way of profits.

Social history can also be notoriously difficult to portray, particularly when depicting historical practices which today's audiences find uncomfortable to witness and are unwilling to remember. To return to Colonial Williamsburg, one of the earliest criticisms leveled at the site was its lack of Black interpreters when the majority of the town's population during that period were Black slaves (Anderson 1980). Even today this type of representation has proved difficult as few people welcome the idea of being employed as a full-time slaves and debate continues around how best to re-create this dimension of Williamsburg without perpetuating the legacy of the racial divide.

A combination of multimedia and living history do, at first sight seem to offer a way out of this dilemma. The former allowing individual exploration of a subject area, including both exciting action and facts, the latter again offering this facility but with the added attractions of the theater. But it is important to look at these media both in terms of what they can offer in the way of education and entertainment and the problems arising from their indiscriminate use in a commercially oriented heritage industry. Living history has often been attacked as being impossibly unauthentic, and it is true that historically many sites did, and still do, have problems addressing these issues. Multimedia, on the other hand, through the legitimizing function of technology, is not seen as so problematic in that context. But how much more authentic or real is multimedia history? It is true that multimedia presentation means that no one perspective on a period need take precedent over another. There is the opportunity to present as many theories as there are academics, but all this derives from technology and it is widely acknowledged that both the technology and its application is predominantly controlled by certain, often commercially oriented elements within society. Where, then, is the reality in multimedia history, or would it be more accurate to ask whose reality?

As tourism replaces heavy industries around Britain they are often replaced by Heritage sites, many of which have a living history element. The employment terms in the heritage industry, in common with most in the service sector, are not good, particularly when compared with the older industries. The work is often part time or seasonal, not offering sufficient money to support a family nor requiring written qualifications. Employers often target women with young children who have little choice but to accept whatever conditions are offered or, increasingly, graduates unable to find other work. However a significant number of employees are taken from the industries around which the sites are based; for example redundant coal face workers acting as tour guides around the Rhondda Heritage Centre, or local people who have had an ongoing interest in a particular period or site. And this local input is probably the most important potential of Living History. The possibility is there for local people who have some first hand or family knowledge of the traditions and folklore of the community to contribute to the visitors experience.

Multimedia on the other hand, although it offers unparalleled opportunities to present vast amounts of information is an interesting fashion, is a centralized form of knowledge. Until these systems become truly interactive, and allow a high level of input from the user as well as an interesting guided tour, the knowledge will always be that of the 'expert' and the designer who created the software. The costs of software involved necessarily results in a limited number of editions, which can never be truly 'local' and so become a form of centralized 'truth', stripped of much of the human local element which was so vital to the community which is being described.

The other issues which must be raised around the application of multimedia technology in museums are around the artifacts themselves. Historical conservation has become an important force in town planning and resource exploitation. If an artifact can be captured in all its various and multifaceted detail on video, which, with the use of fractals in computer generated images, is becoming increasingly possible, will there be any need for the artifact itself? Will the computer image become more real than reality? What need is there for the real thing when its detailed image can be beamed all over the world to be viewed by the smallest child?

And the same thing could apply to living history. Most of the artifacts used on these sites are reproductions. The people themselves mere simulations although this time made of flesh and blood rather than pixels on a screen. The cultures they represent and interpret are make-believe, the characters put away at the end of the day. For an historical period this is obviously an insoluble dilemma, there are no seventeenth-century retainers left to staff Llancaiach Fawr, but in a slightly different setting the implications of simulations replacing the reality soon become clear. Why bother to preserve elements of a culture if it can be stored on CD or re-enacted by interpreters so much more efficiently than the real thing. The lives and culture of the Amazonian Indians offer important insights into the ways of the exotic other and it would be a tragedy if the stories and traditions of their culture were lost, but if these can be captured for posterity like a butterfly on a pin there is no reason to stop cutting down the forests and destroying the people because at the end of the day we can establish a theme park, put them in a museum to interpret their culture and beam the results around the world via the multimedia experience.

This may seem a little far fetched and hyperbolic but this is, in effect, the potential of multimedia and living history. The former can capture the physical entity, the latter the social. Witness the events in Cades Cove, an East Tennessee community which became a living history museum soon after the Great Smokies National Park was established. The families who had remained on their land were given notice to quit or had to accept employment with the National Park Service as living exhibits (Dunn 1988). I dare say that somewhere their agricultural techniques, religious beliefs, and in fact many aspects of their folklore are preserved for posterity on computer but, in essence, Cades Cove, the community, is gone replaced by a Heritage site. As for the plight of the Amazonian Indians, there is no need to worry, for their future has been assured by Virgin, who, alongside their travel destination databases (which they plan to manufacture with the help of Phillips) and world travel simulations, have released Living in the Rainforest (Beckett, 1990), an interactive videodisc project aimed at developing cultural empathy with a population faced with the wholesale destruction of their environment partially financed by a greedy, technology-dependent Northern Hemisphere.

But it is not all bad news. What both living history and multimedia can offer is the experience of the other without invading the space of the other. For example interactive multimedia is being put to good use in educating social workers, allowing them to confront problems within ethnic minority populations they may encounter in the course of their work (Falk *et al.* 1990). This program combines some of the best elements of both living history type role playing and interactive multimedia and, although operated through a computer, allow the student to enter another culture, learn about it, and make mistakes, all without impinging on a social group who have already learned to distrust the ethno-centricity of the authorities. They could also allow the twenty-first century tourist to 'visit' some of the more obscure but increasingly popular locations currently being marketed to the 'genuine traveller' but ultimately destined to become tomorrow's Costa del Sol.

They can also arouse the interests of a generation with a jaded palate for reality, reared on Disney and the Terminator, where fantasy life is so much more interesting than what you can find in books. And this is an important factor. The entertainment industry has the habit of appealing to our weaknesses and children are often the first to accept the message. It is virtually impossible to convince a child that reading can be fun if they've been told that computer games are better. So the obvious answer is to put the contents of a book into a game. Alternatively you can allow them to take part in the game, hear the language from the lips of a real person, dress in the costumes, and handle the weaponry. In effect multimedia and living history can act as foils for each other, each exploiting the other's weaknesses and providing increasing depth of understanding and knowledge to a wider audience through their dual roles of entertainment and teaching.

The nexus around which this revolves in both mediums is the *potentiality* for interaction, whether between machine and user or interpreter and visitor. Interestingly it is at this point where living history seems to fall down, whereas the computer demands a level of response from its user and that response can, in most cases be given in private, the interpreter has, to a large extent, to rely on the good will of the visitor in order to make the interaction work. Consequently they do tend to 'pick' on a cooperative person and these sorts of demands have been known to make quivering wrecks of the most forthright of people.

However it is not all roses in the multimedia garden either. True interactivity is still some way away, although Hypertext is starting to make in-roads into the problem. The heart of the matter is that only when the user can contribute to and change the software with which she/he is interacting and those changes are reflected in subsequent users interactions with the system will a state of true interactivity have been reached.

So it is this claim to interactivity, this potentiality of communication, which may allow a true exchange of information and opinion between people and between machines and users, that connects these two mediums of transmission. And makes both worth fighting to improve. The important factor to remember is that as things stand at the moment both interactive multimedia designers and living history sites are often operating under a profit-making policy, not that there is anything intrinsically wrong with that. Where the problem arises is when profit is allowed to dictate content and where the bank balance is considered more important than any pretense to reality.

The *possibilities* of this future, however, are mind blowing, its advantages to our crowded skies and roads and increasingly hard-pressed environment are obvious and personally I am looking forward to a future that could allow me to go anywhere and meet anybody without having to go though customs. But, as has been said before, the ramifications of this future on political, cultural, and social structures are numerous and in many cases fraught with dangers. With 20/20 hindsight it is possible to critically examine the far reaching effects of the industrial revolution, indeed this retrospective analysis has kept many generations of historians and sociologists off the streets. Faced with what could be an equally influential, and possibly destructive change in society but this time armed with the experiences and lessons learnt it should be possible to approach this change better informed than our forebears hopefully with happier consequences. For there is no going back, although it is possible that in the years to come our living, breathing interpreters will be replaced by virtual ones behind the head set and it does seem that the future we are looking into may contain more pixels than persons and more software than sites.

Together, interactive multimedia and living history could offer opportunities in education and entertainment which would allow people to gain deeper insight into their world, past and present, although for my part I concur with the words of David Kekone of the Otis College of Art and Design, a man with a vested interest in the continuing computer revolution, but with an interesting insight into the complexity of the issues involved. He says:

> Ultimately what all this comes down to, all this incredibly complex math and fast computers, is communication between people, something that is not technologically advanced at all ... [for] no matter how fast the computer or how good the math, it will never be able to match what happens when you look into another person's eyes.[1]

REFERENCES

Anderson, J. 1982. Living History: Simulating Everyday Life in Living Museums. *American Quarterly* 34:290–306.

[1]David Kekone of the Otis College of Art and Design, on The Net, an Illuminations production for BBC Education, 1994.

Beckett, W. 1990. Facing the Future—a publishers' perspective. In *The Interactive Learning Revolution: Multimedia in Education and Training*, ed. J. Barker and R. Tucker. London: Kogan Page.

Dunn, D. 1988. *Cades Cove: the Life and Death of a Southern Appalachian Community*. Knoxville: University of Tennessee Press.

Falk, D. *et al*. 1990. Interactive Technology Impacts on Increasing Culture Awareness in Education for the Human Services. *Computers in Human Services* 7:265–76.

Martlew, R. 1990. Multi-media in Museums: Potential Applications of Interactive Technology. *Society of Museum Archeologists Journal*, 44–52.

Tucker, R., ed. 1989. *Interactive Media: The Human Issues*. London: Kogan Page.

Folklore in Use 2, 25–36 (1994)

Folklore on Film

John D. Niles

By offering a conference on the "The Marketing of Tradition", the Folklore Society has presented an appealing exercise in incongruity. Tradition implies conservation and heritage, does it not? Old men with whiskers, scythes and stories; old women with looms. Marketing, in the minds of most Americans at least, is likely to call up a picture of young, beautiful and ruthless people manipulating glossy images for profit. The *marketing* of *tradition*: what do these two things have in common?

In its actual workings, of course, tradition is no disinterested enterprise that remains abstracted from the economy of consumerism. As Eric Hobsbawm and other historians have remarked (Hobsbawm and Ranger 1991), tradition is no hypostatic entity, timeless and self-perpetuating. Many traditions are of recent and decidedly human invention and some of them—think of Christmas gifts, or the American Halloween—have a notorious relation to commercial factors.

In general, marketing not only *can* have something to do with tradition; it regularly *does*. It *has* done for as long as we can think back into the past. It is impossible to think about the folktales of the Brothers Grimm, for example, without also taking into account the history of that artifact, the *Kinder- und Hausmärchen*, that in its various editions and translations is one of the phenomenal successes of commercial book production. Whether sold as a book or appropriated as part of the marketing of almost innumerable byproducts, from movies to stuffed dwarves to fabulous theme parks, the Grimms' collection has surely generated a higher mountain of gold that was ever guarded by a fairytale dragon.

Film, by its nature, is an expensive medium that depends for its existence on rather complex marketing factors. Whereas folklore itself, as a general rule, is free, a film that takes as its subject some aspect of folk tradition requires big money to produce. In its early stages it needs sponsors, and when complete it needs to attract consumers as well, whether through commercial movie theatres or through educational television networks, schools, or universities.

Commercially speaking, to call a film a "documentary" is often to give it the kiss of death. The chief practical problem that confronts a filmmaker who wishes to document some aspect of folk culture is the question: "How do I make it marketable?" This subject is not a crass one, for it dovetails with the issues of artistic integrity and appeal: "How can I arrive at a final product that is strong enough to stand on its own as something that discerning people will go out of their way to see?"

To illustrate the full range of filmmakers' responses to this question would take some time. My purpose here is to draw attention to three films that represent successful fusions of art and marketability. Each presents a different vision of twentieth-century American folk culture. Each carries the distinctive stamp of its maker, three observers of the contemporary scene whose work I happen to admire: *Being a Joines: A Life in the Brushy Mountains*, by Tom Davenport of Delaplane, Virginia; *J'ai été au bal*, by Les Blank of El Cerrito, California; and *Road Scholar*, a film whose guiding spirit is Andrei Codrescu of New Orleans, Louisiana. None of these three films will ever make a mountain of gold. Each, still, is able to present an image of American folklife that departs strikingly from glossy stereotypes promoted by the culture industries.

BEING A JOINES

Being a Joines takes its title from the name of the person who holds center stage in this film, John E. Joines of Wilkes County, North Carolina (b. 1914). At an early age Joines was given the nickname "Frail" because he was anything but feeble. During his childhood he learned how to earn respect in new situations by using his fists to whip anyone who challenged him. On his eighteenth birthday he won a bet by carrying five hundred pounds of feed around a store building, one sack under each arm, one on each shoulder, and one grasped in his teeth. But Frail Joines turns out to be no mere burly, blue-eyed country boy. As his life story unfolds through successive filmed interviews, with marvelous examples of his tall tales and personal-experience narratives, a life of humor, dignity and grace unfolds.

The film's subtitle, *A Life in the Brushy Mountains*, anchors Joines to the particular region of the eastern Blue Ridge Mountains in which he has lived all of his life with the exception of three years in the US Army during World War II. One of Davenport's aims in this film is to show how the major social and economic changes that affected this part of Appalachia during the earlier part of this century are reflected in the life and narrative repertory of this person. When Joines was a child he lived on a subsistence farm, like most of his neighbors. By the time he joined the Army the older rural economy had come nearly to a halt. Many farms had gone back to wasteland, as happened in other parts of

America when the horse economy, with its need for extensive hayfields, gave way to the automobile economy and increasing urbanization. Many rural people sought out jobs in factories or service industries at the same time as intensive forestry and mining emptied the hills of game.

Joines' years with the Allied forces in Europe affected him profoundly, with their images of unprecedented brutality. After his discharge Joines returned to his native North Carolina to work as an auto mechanic. On Easter Sunday 1971, inspired by the revivalism that was sweeping the region, Joines underwent a religious reconversion, and since that time he and his wife Blanche have lived a life centered on charismatic religion and on the particular evangelical movement known as the Sons of God. In the latter part of the film, Blanche, who previously is given no speaking role, comes increasingly to share center stage with her husband. As the camera shifts to encompass the two of them, we witness the power with which the Joines' spirituality has brought them together in their later years.

In a study guide that accompanies this film (Newman *et al.* 1981),[1] Davenport makes clear that the film was not an easy one to make. When he started work on it in 1975, it was to be no more than a 15-minute presentation of a few of Joines' tall tales and comic anecdotes. Five years and much footage later, it ended as a 55-minute-long exploration of Joines as a man, as seen chiefly through his own storytelling. Through this shift of purpose, Joines becomes in part the shaper of the film, not just its passive subject. As it stands, the film takes its form not from preconceived generic categories (such as the tall tale) but from a free-flowing, sympathetic collaboration between Joines as storyteller and Davenport as audience, friend, cameraman, and editor. The film powerfully demonstrates how what we call personal identity is largely a function of storytelling. Through the examples of a man and a woman filmed in a situation of mutual trust, we see an enactment of the principle that the stories that people tell create them, in a sense, as sentient individuals grounded in a particular place and time.

The making of *Being a Joines* thus has a plot to it that parallels the plot of Joines' own life. Davenport invites us to contemplate the film's history from his initial plan, to the traumatic breakdown of this plan, to the final happy resolution—a resolution that was celebrated by all of Joines' family, as well as by Davenport and his collaborators at the University of North Carolina, Chapel Hill, at the film's initial screening in 1980.

---

[1]Copies of the study guide are available from Davenport films. Newman, one of the Joines' two daughters, was an important liaison for the project through her work toward the MA degree in Folklore at Chapel Hill.

In the film, Joines' life proceeds from simplicity, through adversity, to grace. The simplicity is that of his good-old-boy origins in a culture of subsistence farmers, fox-hunters, moonshiners, brawlers, and raconteurs.[2] The adversity is that entailed by modernization, with its attendant demons of war and dehumanization. For nearly twenty-five years after World War II, as Joines remarks, "it was hard for me to even believe that there was a God" (Newman *et al.* 1981:8). The third period of Joines' life begins only in his late forties with his acceptance of Christ as his personal Savior. At this point, thanks to the inspirational example of his wife, Joines' exceptional physical strength finds its counterpart in inner fortitude. As he remarks at one point with customary directness, "Me and the Lord's a majority in any crowd" (Newman *et al.* 1981:38).

With its length of 55 minutes, this film is targeted for the medium of educational television. It was produced with the aid of grants provided to the North Carolina Arts Council and the Institute for Southern Studies and is marketed as one of four films in The American Traditional Culture Series, a joint production of Tom Davenport films and the Curriculum in Folklore of the University of North Carolina, Chapel Hill.[3]

J'AI ÉTÉ AU BAL

Les Blank's *J'ai été au bal* is a longer and more expensive feature film that is meant as a tribute to the Cajuns of southern Louisiana and their style of dance music. It is directed chiefly to the independent film market,

---

[2] It is one of the strengths of the film that this rural past is not depicted simply in nostalgic tones, although there is regret at the passing of some of its features. Joines' father was an alcholic, for example, and Frail speaks of how he used to hate him; Frail left home and never lived with his father after he turned thirteen.

[3] The other films in the series are *The Shakers*, a historical overview of this religious group and its songs, dances and communal society; *Born for Hard Luck*, a portrait of the black medicine-show performer Arthur "Peg-Leg Sam" Jackson; and *A Singing Stream: A Black Family Chronicle*, a celebration of the Landis family of Granville County, North Carolina. Study booklets for these last two films are available from the filmmaker. Davenport has also produced a series of nine dramatizations of folktales of the Brothers Grimm in rural Appalachian dress, one film on country music and two on fox hunting.

where Blank has scored some success.[4] The music from its sound track has been released separately.[5] The film includes extended footage of such giants of the Cajun and zydeco scene as Michael Doucet, Clifton Chenier, Dewey Balfa, Marc Savoy, and Dennis McGee, supplemented by still shots of the stars of earlier generations as well. The values that the film honors modulate away from stoicism, endurance, wit and quiet faith—the qualities of a Joines—in favor of something more ebullient. The film celebrates the kind of spirit that lifts you off the ground and gets your feet moving.

Blank's fondness for garlic, hot pepper, music, dance and laughter is evident in many of his films and this is no exception. As one reviewer has written, he likes to document "the lost art of having a good time" (Patowski 1980). At the same time, Blank maintains a steady hand on the camera and a scholar's precision about details. He puts Cajun music into an historical perspective that reveals the complex interplay of French-speaking, English-speaking and Spanish-speaking cultures in the Deep South, never losing sight of the contribution of African-Americans to creole culture, with their blues and field hollers. Blank is comfortable letting the camera settle on speakers for periods of time that would never be tolerated in mainstream films, and he lets people tell their own stories: of the stigma of speaking French in the 1930s, for example, or of the effect of military service during World War II in making Cajuns aware of the distinctiveness of their regional culture.

Since I have heard Blank taken to task for his tendency to link the apparently unrelated subjects of music and food, it is interesting to see how one of the musicians highlighted here, Marc Savoy, connects the two subjects. After demonstrating the basic seven-note scale of his accordion, Savoy adds a bit of ornament to give the music "that secret ingredient that makes it taste like a Cajun sauce." Shifting his figure of speech, he then adds other embellishments that, he says, are "like the lace on the dress." Later in the same scene, when speaking of Dennis McGee's legendary fiddle playing, he remarks on the impossibility of imitating

[4]He has had retrospectives at FILMEX (1977), Minneapolis (1978), New York (1979), London (1982), Mexico City (1984), Paris (1986), San Diego (1989), Augsburg (1990), Vienna (1992) and Los Angeles (1992); and is the recipient of numerous awards including the British Academy Award for Best Feature Documentary, 1982 (for *Burden of Dreams*, on German filmmaker Werner Herzog).

[5]An accompanying sound track recording, available on either two CDs or two cassettes, has been produced by Chris Strachwitz of Arhoolie Records, El Cerrito, California.

that style of music on his accordion, with its seven-tone scale: "we just don't have the words to tell that story." For Savoy as for Les Blank, music-making, cooking, dress, and storytelling are parts of a single cultural system whose analogous elements are naturally linked through metaphor.

Blank has now produced about twenty films documenting traditional American music. Four of these feature Cajun or zydeco music (the others are *Spend it All, Dry Wood* and *Hot Pepper*); two are studies of Black Texas bluesmen (*The Blues Accordin' to Lightnin' Hopkins* and *A Well Spent Life*, a portrait of Mance Lipscomb); two document Norteña or Tex-Mex music of the Southwest border (*Chulas Fronteras* and *Del Mero Corazon*); one evokes the New Orleans festival of Mardi Gras (*Always for Pleasure*); one celebrates traditional Appalachian fiddler Tommy Jarrell (*Sprout Wings and Fly*); one features Serbian-Americans and their music (*Živeli: Medicine for the Heart*); and one presents a delightfully detached view of Middle American polkamania (*In Heaven There Is No Beer?*). Others of Blank's films have titles as inviting as their subjects are improbable: *Gap-Toothed Women*, a series of interviews of women who have in common just one thing, and *Garlic is as Good as Ten Mothers*, on the highbrow and lowbrow culture of one of the civilized world's most notorious foods.

With his total opus—and I have not cited a number of other films he has made—Les Blank has gained a reputation as one of America's best independent filmmakers, and folklorists can be thankful that he has chosen to specialize in this field. His films have a populist bias that goes hand-in-hand with an indifference to the white-collar world of WASP-ish America.[6] Among Blank's accomplishments is that he is the inventor of SmellaRound, his down-home counterpart to Cinerama. This is a marketing technique whereby he prepares a large pot of red rice and beans in the theater while the film is being shown. Free samples are given out afterwards. For Blank, this is a typical gesture toward the idea of participatory culture. I have the impression that he will not consider one of his music films truly successful until his audience literally dance in the aisles. Besides being the name of a well-known Cajun song, the title of his film *J'ai été au bal* is perhaps a personal statement. "I went to the dance, "he seems to be saying: "me, Les Blank, the filmmaker, and you can believe *I* had a good time."

---

[6]One of Blank's first independent films, *God Respects Us When We Work, but Loves Us When We Dance*, is devoted to the Easter Sunday Love-In held in Los Angeles in 1967. "I find my own cultural heritage to be ... uh ... a bit thin," he has remarked to one journalist (Hoberman 1979).

ROAD SCHOLAR

Somewhat like Les Blank put on fast-forward but with a cooler, almost surrealist vision, Andrei Codrescu introduces us to a number of out-of-the-way folk groups and quirky individuals in his 1993 film *Road Scholar*. This is a feature-length film that required considerable financial backing to produce.[7] A trade book under the same title has been released in both hard cover and paperback with Codrescu's droll text and a set of fine photos by David Graham (Codrescu 1992). This book is not Codrescu's first publishing venture by any means. He is the author of some twenty-five books, including *Diapers on the Snow, The History of the Growth of Heaven, The Marriage of Insult and Injury* and *Necrocorrida* (these are all poetry); *The Muse is Always Half-Dressed in New Orleans* and *Raised by Puppets, Only to Be Killed by Research* (critical essays); and *The Life and Times of an Involuntary Genius* (this is autobiography, of course). Codrescu has edited *American Poetry Since 1970: Up Late*, an anthology of poetry by authors who have published chiefly in little-known literary magazines. He is well known as a commentator on National Public Radio. But *Road Scholar*, as both book and movie, is his most ambitious commercial enterprise to date.

This commercial angle may seem an anomaly on the part of an author who has railed frequently against the organized marketing of images that is the hallmark of capitalism: "the McDonaldization of American culture," as he has put it. But as a surrealist poet, Codrescu could be said to have made a career out of paradoxes.[8]

In *Road Scholar* he retraces, as a grown man, his own literal and spiritual footsteps from the time when he first arrived in the United States having left his native Romania in 1965 at age nineteen. The title of the film serves as one of several tributes to Jack Kerouac's novel *On the Road*. It also invokes a genre of commercial film and literature often

---

[7]Through Roger Weisburg of Public Policy Productions, associated with WNET, New York.

[8]One unintended paradox is perhaps worth noting. In the introduction to the poetry anthology just mentioned, Codrescu speaks somewhat scornfully of the mainstream American poet who is married, has two kids, has received a prestigious government arts award, and teaches at a university where he edits a literary magazine. Codrescu himself is married and teaches at Louisiana State University, where he edits a literary magazine named *Exquisite Corpse*—an apt evocation of his Transylvanian roots. Contradiction has never worried him, as he is the first to admit.

known as "road movies" or "road novels", one type of which is summed up by the film *Road Warrior*, with its images of running gunbattles fought by itinerant hero Mel Gibson. Unlike Gibson, Codrescu is anything but an action hero. He makes a rather large joke of the fact that before making this film, he had never learned how to drive a car—a disability that expresses an ideological stance. But there is another play on words in the film's title as well, for surely *Road Scholar* is a subversion of *Rhodes Scholar* (the designate for members of a program aimed at athletic scholars). If you searched for adjectives to describe Codrescu, neither 'scholarly' nor 'athletic' would leap to mind. Still, he is an incisive scholar of the contemporary American scene. Here he seems to take on the role of an 'anti-Rhodes Scholar', tracing out a narrative that takes him from Europe to America and to the sites not of an elite tradition but rather of a humming popular culture.

The film is so encompassing that its contents would be impossible to summarize here in detail. It begins in New Orleans, where Codrescu acquires a suitable car for his pilgrimage—a candy-apple-red 1968 Cadillac convertible—and makes a frightening attempt to learn how to drive it. The journey proper begins in Manhattan, where he pays homage to Allen Ginsburg, visits Ellis Island and the Statue of Liberty, and speaks with some homeless Haitian immigrants. After a stop at the grave of Walt Whitman, he goes on to visit the Bruderhof (a Christian utopian community in upstate New York) and the Oneida mansion, the former center of a more upscale style of utopian community. A few scenes follow in Detroit, the mecca of the religion of the automobile as well as the place of his first residence in America, but now in large part an urban wasteland. Codrescu proceeds to Chicago and visits (among other sites of interest) a Roller Skating Gospel Rink where black Christians worship the God of rollerskates. Proceeding west, he stops off to visit a top-of-the-line cattle auction and to take machine-gun shooting lessons from a woman named Bo, whose husband runs a Survivalist store. Bo, for whom "to be an American, in America, owning machine-guns is the best thing in the world," teaches her pupils in three different garbs—fatigues, a bikini, or nude—for three different fees. Codrescu then treats us to a whirlwind tour of New Age New Mexico, the womb of countless cults and communes. He visits a retirement community in Sun City, Arizona and films its resident band, a punk-rock group whose lead singer is an attractive aging Italian-American female ex-mortician dressed in leather miniskirt and high heels. After an obligatory stop in Las Vegas, with its high-stakes gamblers and its Little White Chapel Drive-Up Wedding Window, Codrescu eventually concludes his odyssey in San Francisco with scenes at City Lights Bookstore (heart of the Beat counterculture of the 1950s) and at Ocean Beach, where he ruminates about the improbable, hugely incompatible ingredients that were "thrown into the boiling cauldron of this continent," where very little in the great melting pot actually melted; for here "languages, people, habits, cuisines, mores ... and beliefs continue undaunted side by side" (1992:193).

CONCLUSIONS

Each of these three films is the product of a personal vision. Each departs markedly from standard commercial representations of American culture, and the picture that each offers is a value-laden one.

Davenport's film would lose much of its edge if viewers were not aware that for decades, the Frail Joinses in our society have been subject to almost ludicrous stereotyping on the part of those media interests who have capitalized on the image of the Appalachian hill folk.[9] His film is a kind of cultural critique, and the implied subject of this criticism is the willingness of outsiders to accept ready-made images of this regional culture—whether of the bigoted redneck, the backwoods raconteur, the gauche hillbilly, or the Bible-thumping fundamentalist—without listening to the lives of real people.

While Les Blank's *J'ai été au bal* is not less an act of cultural critique, the target of this critique is somewhat broader, for Blank's films tend to define themselves in unspoken opposition to the whole of mainstream, mass-mediated culture in America. By offering up the joyous sounds of Cajun music, with its attendant dancing, feasting, and conviviality, Blank gives us a vision of heaven. His films do this again and again. They uplift us by offering the assurance that not all of America is McDonaldized, nor is all of it a gray Puritan legacy of rules, duties, and responsibilities. It would be ungrateful, perhaps, for his reviewers to point out that Cajuns too have rules and duties. They too may sometimes take their culture from a can. For the point of Blank's film is not just to document life as it is, but to proclaim or prophesy life as it might be in some transcendent realm where life is a dance and God plays the fiddle.

If both of these films are value-laden, the same is even more true of *Road Scholar*, despite Codrescu's steady posture of bemused outsider in a society that defies rational understanding. As the film progresses, his detached stance turns out to be a concealed weapon, for in scene after scene he comes face to face with Americans whose sincerity about themselves and their own particular culture is nothing short of

---

[9]For an incisive overview of the ways in which Appalachia has been subject to image-making over the years (by folklorists, among others) see Whisnant 1983.

staggering. By point and counterpoint, Codrescu works into his film two large sets of alternative values: on one side is a sequence of visionary artists headed by Ginsburg and the ghost of Whitman, and on the other side is Kowalski's sausage factory in Detroit. The artificial neatness of this set of oppositions is then accentuated by Codrescu's wickedly ironic undermining of a range of post-hippy dropouts and New Age gurus and spiritual healers. While no aspect of American culture is immune to his ironies, Codrescu makes clear where his basic sympathies lie. Like Lawrence Ferlinghetti, poet and former publisher of City Lights Books, Codrescu apparently looks forward to the day when "the citizens will plant great gardens on the freeways, and that'll be that".[10] Once every Cadillac is planted with its own private garden, he and his friends will pass effortlessly along the underground passageways that connect Café Trieste in San Francisco, California, with Café Maria in Sibiu, Romania, and every child will be a poet.

None of the films I have discussed is above criticism. *Being a Joines* might have gained in clarity if the filmmaker had been willing to insert himself more openly into the interview situation—although with a crew that consisted of just himself as cameraman plus one sound man, there is virtually no way that Davenport could have done this. As things stand, we infer his presence as Joines' chief audience, but we can only guess at what interactions occur between them. *J'ai été au bal* shows skill in camerawork that is perhaps not consistently matched by skill in editing. The strength of the film lies in its images of the people who make the music. Since there is no story to it apart from the evolution of Cajun music and culture over time, from the era of traditional fiddling to that of electric swamp rock, the film may go on a bit long for viewers who are not already addicted to the Cajun scene. *Road Scholar* differs from the other two films in its reliance on a narrator who interacts with the people being interviewed. It is from this dual vision, the insider's and the outsider's, that the film gains much of its comic edge. Codrescu's presence is essential, for what the film attempts to portray is not just the "given" American cultural landscape; it is also the new configuration that arises when a free-thinking anarchistic immigrant poet like Codrescu enters upon the scene. Insofar as the film attempts to delineate existing folk cultures, it does so at too bewildering a pace for any of them to be known with intimacy. We are left with an impression of zaniness and great plenitude, but as in most real-life journeys, the impression is a blurred one based on many places seen too quickly.

Despite such incidental criticisms, each of these films is a refreshing

---

[10]Ferlinghetti, quoted in Codrescu 1992:184.

and even sometimes a masterful piece of work. Taken together, they reveal sides of America that have almost wholly escaped the attention of the mass media. Particularly for people abroad, whose images of the current scene in America may be derived chiefly from glossy media sources like "Dallas" and "Beverly Hills Cop" or from package tours to prefabricated tourist spots,[11] any of these films could function as a reality check. Davenport shows us a single strong individual in the rooted rural tradition. Blank celebrates a Southern regional culture that has refused to be assimilated to anglophone norms. Codrescu opens our eyes to an evolving *fin-de-siècle* America, prone to spiritualisms of various sorts, where the dialectics of freedom and repression are operating at hothouse temperatures. In each film we see abundant evidence of the free, creative spirit that—invisible as it tends to be—is still characteristic of the private life of many people living off the beaten track.

REFERENCES

Codrescu, Andrei. 1992. *Road Scholar: Coast to Coast Late in the Century.* With photographs by David Graham. New York: Hyperion.
Hoberman, J. 1979. Les Blank Retrospective. *The Village Voice* (June 25).
Hobsbawm, Eric and Terence Ranger, eds. 1991. *The Invention of Tradition.* Cambridge: Cambridge University Press.
Newman, Joyce Joines, Daniel W. Patterson, Allen Tullos and Tom Davenport. 1991. *Being a Joines, A Life in the Brushy Mountains: Background, Transcription, and Commentary.* Chapel Hill: The Curriculum in Folklore, The University of North Carolina at Chapel Hill.
Patoski, Joe Nick. 1980. Let the Good Times Roll. *Texas Monthly* (April).
Whisnant, David E. 1983. *All That is Native and Fine: The Politics of Culture in an American Region.* Chapel Hill: University of North Carolina Press.

[11]By "prefabricated" tourist spots I mean safe ones that resemble a Hollywood stage set. There is evidence that in my own part of the country, chiefly in response to a perceived rise in street violence, Japanese tourism (a major factor in the economy) is now increasingly restricted to spots like Disneyland and Las Vegas.

FILMOGRAPHY

Being a Joines: A Life in the Brushy Mountains, a film by Tom Davenport. Fifty-five minutes. 16 mm rental, $60.00; 16 mm sale, $800.00; VHS/Beta sale, $90.00. Available from Davenport Films, RR1, Box 527, Delaplane, VA 22025, USA.

J'ai été au bal, a film by Les Blank and Maureen Gosling. Eighty-four minutes. ½" or ¾" video, VHS or Beta format, $49.95; for PAL format $59.95. Available from Flower Films, 10341 San Pablo Avenue, El Cerrito, CA 94530, USA.

Road Scholar, featuring Andrei Codrescu. Produced and directed by Roger Weisburg for Samuel Goldwyn Films, with camerawork by Jean de Segonzac. Seventy-five minutes. Not available on video (June 1994).

Folklore in Use 2, 37–41 (1994)

Historical Drama in Historic Houses: Sketches from New South Wales

Ann Berriman

The Historic Houses Trust of New South Wales and the National Trust conserve key sites associated with the history of Australia, integrating them with the local surroundings and society by staging contemporary exhibitions and events. The houses, administration buildings, grazing properties, farms and gardens are open to the public. The Trust bodies, through their education programmes, material and presentation, aim to disseminate information about the changing social fabric of Australia. Since the White Australia Policy was abandoned in the late 1960s, and with our new-found Multiculturalism, people of many nationalities have made their home in Australia. They come from all European nations, from the Pacific area, from Africa, India, Middle East, from North and South America, and most recently from Asia.

There is, consequently, a need to consider this fact in marketing our heritage. The Trust emphasizes participatory programmes especially for schools and other educational institutions. I believe that familiarizing the young with various aspects of past history and, in the case of Australia, an awareness of the delicate balance of our ecology both links them to the present and is relevant to the future preservation of heritage and of the land itself. Stemming from the early days of British settlement, trends in agricultural development in raising cattle and sheep and introducing new species of flora and fauna (e.g. the rabbit and the fox) set the pattern for Australia's ecologically ill-considered development.

The damage done to the soil by running huge herds of cattle and sheep, and the erosion caused by clearing of the unique and extraordinary rainforests is now virtually irretrievable. My point here is that Australian heritage is as much landscape as historic buildings and that we should be preserving all the areas that remain, as we have with Kakadu, a large tract in the Northern Territory, which includes ranges, gorges, lakes, etc., and the Daintree rainforest, in Queensland.

Our heritage building sites range from mansions of notable figures of the colonial period to public buildings such as old Government House at Parramatta (16 miles from Sydney) and Hyde Park Barracks (in the center of modern Sydney) which were built by Lachlan Macquarie, Governor of New South Wales from 1810–1822. Many of the buildings and churches of Sydney were designed by the convict architect Francis Greenway, appointed by Macquarie, and remain today architecturally noteworthy. As has happened in many cities, development has dictated that many buildings be demolished and concrete and glass edifices now stand in their place. However, for us in Australia, there were fewer to start with than in older parts of the world, so the loss is particularly keenly felt.

The programmes that I devise for the Art Gallery of New South Wales and the Historic Houses Trust involve contemporary writers, poets, artists and musicians, as well as the dramatization of history utilizing specific sites such as Vaucluse House, the Royal Botanic Gardens, Old Government House and the Hyde Park Barracks.

I was approached by the curator of Vaucluse House, a mansion set in 12 hectares of garden, the only surviving Sydney harbor-side estate, with a request to work on a series of programmes for their calendar of events involving writers and readings. I had just attended a reading of Alex Buzo's play *Macquarie* which I considered to be an appropriate piece for production. I envisaged it as a dramatized reading utilizing the reception, stables and courtyard of the mansion (Vaucluse House) as locations with the audience moving from place to place.

Subsequently Alex Buzo offered to direct the work and then two prominent actors indicated a keenness to be involved, so suddenly it became a full-scale production. Not without a great deal of organization: staging, lighting, props and costumes. It quickly became apparent to me that the evocation of historical characters in a mansion of the period created an exceptional atmosphere, a time-warp, imbuing the environ- ment with the very personalities of the characters.

Macquarie replaced the notorious Governor Bligh, of Mutiny on the *Bounty* fame in 1810. He inherited the turmoil of the comparatively new settlement: its corruption; soldiers made surly by the enforcement of martial law to counteract the Rum Rebellion; the problems surrounding the Aboriginals who were in turn affected by drink and disease, both introduced to them by the white population. Added to this was the religious and ethical influence of the questionable Reverend Samuel Marsden who believed that the convicts were irredeemable and that the Aboriginals, savages as he thought them, were of no consequence. Macquarie did much to shape the new society by insisting that convicts were people not just recalcitrant felons. Consequently he tried to rehabilitate them by granting them their freedom and tickets-of-leave (that is, a convict was given his liberty under certain restrictions before his sentence had expired). To the dismay of the Home Office in London and the Reverend Marsden, Macquarie appointed the convict Francis

Greenway as colonial architect, and together with Elizabeth Macquarie, they designed many elegant and substantial buildings.

Alex Buzo presents Macquarie as a humane man in a complex social and political situation, working against forces that ultimately resulted in his downfall and his recall to England. The play deals with all these elements most eloquently and provides a base for further exploration of Australian history as it is not only entertaining but informative. Parallels can be drawn with recent Australian political history (the sacking of Prime Minister Gough Whitlam in 1975) which give greater emphasis to the colonial problems, and provide modern relevance for the play.

Following a substantial and influential review, the word spread and we played to full houses for a week, that is, audiences of about 110—all that would fit in the courtyard where the play was finally staged.

Because of its success the play was produced at three more sites, Old Government House at Parramatta, Hyde Park Barracks and the Royal Botanic Gardens, all actually associated with Macquarie and his governing of the colony.

The performances take on greater significance and immediacy by being directly related to the historic surroundings. When the character Greenway describes his visions for proposed buildings, when Macquarie walks by the sandstone wall that he had built, when Elizabeth Macquarie speaks of her garden, the historic surroundings are brought to life for the audience, who sit before the very houses and in the very courtyards designed and built by Greenway.

In the outdoor performances the sound effects are generously provided by nature: the screech of cockatoos, the manic laughter of the kookaburra and, in the dusk of evening, the whir of bats' wings among the huge Moreton Bay fig trees adds an element of foreboding to Macquarie's final hours as Governor.

We ran the ninety-minute play without an interval so there was no break in the thread of the narrative, no movement between time past and time present and no diminishing of impact on the audience.

The company was run as a co-operative with the actors taking a percentage of the box office and sharing in the initial grant of $1000 production money given by the Historic Houses Trust. After the first production I established our group of actors as The Company of Others. We have since been approached as a company to perform a play for a specific site: an island in Sydney Harbor.

It was during the production of the sketch in the newly restored Hyde Park Barracks in Macquarie Street—designed by Greenway to house up to 600 convicts—that the curator suggested that more items of an historical nature should be incorporated into their programming in order to take full advantage of the site which retains many archaeological remnants.

As a result I wrote and produced a short play "From the Barracks to Bethnal Green". I based it loosely on letters (later published in England) written by the convict John Slater to his wife in England. It deals with the hardship, the loneliness and the stress of separation provoked by such a distance which, at the time, took at least eight months to span. I found the extracts of the letters interesting because they revealed a man thoughtful about his situation and aware of the events going on around him. The play was presented in the hammock room, the original sleeping quarters for over a hundred convicts. It was performed before a group of people who had been tried in a mock-court and were spending the night in the hammocks as part of a programme of experiencing convict life. The sense of the presence of the men who once slept there inches apart is keenly felt. The play is made even more eerie by being acted by candle-light only, and being prefaced by a sound-scape evoking the anger and pain of the convicts echoing throughout the building. After this harrowing experience the audience, hopefully, falls asleep until they are mustered at dawn for a sail on a tall ship.

Subsequently I also wrote a sketch for children to be incorporated into a three-hour sail on the tall ship *The Solway Lass*. The children interacted with the crew, becoming convicts and sailors, and among their activities, tied knots, sang sea shanties and scrubbed the decks.

The interest lies, I believe, in writing material that is site-specific, evoking the characters of the times and place, and portraying the related events. The action has greater resonance and the material becomes a basis for extension of historical factual interest. The dramatization fixes the images and the information contained in the text.

On the practical side, and an extremely important aspect to consider for anyone producing a play outside the theater, the difficulties encountered in producing a play in a building which is already given over to the daily routine of administration, exhibitions and educational activity are numerous. The advent of a stage crew plus actors can be quite unnerving to members of staff. It is absolutely necessary to have a meeting with all personnel in order that those who are not usually involved in a creative project understand fully that various problems will arise, such as invading staff rooms (which usually become the green room) or general license to what is regarded as sacrosanct. We found in the outside productions of *Macquarie* that other hazards were encountered. Heavy footsteps over gravel, or a truck being driven up the driveway, were in conflict with the drama engaged in the play. So obvious, one might say, yet repeatedly we had to police the environs to protect it from these intrusions.

Through all these experiences I became aware that our past is a rich area that can provide many opportunities for playwrights to reveal particular aspects of history, times, places and people. Fortunately, there are many contemporary and modern sources available which do much to provide an understanding of the context of convict life and the attitudes of those governing the colony. It is difficult in Australia with only two hundred years of history to link into a European past; the closest we can come to our forebears is to envisage them in a Europe which, because of both time and distance, is somewhat alien to us. The galleries and museums of Europe are filled with recognizable landscapes, architecture, and artifacts; simply to walk in the streets is to interact with a very tangible past. In Australia few historic buildings and the artworks of the past in our galleries are also European, but objectified; they manifest themselves as elements from another time and place, not *our* time, not *our* place. We *now* are people of the twentieth century, we *now* are multicultural and are beginning to see ourselves as part of another continent, Asia.

One might then pose the question: Is this focus on Anglo-Celtic history a naive attempt to relate to a really remote past, to validate our beginnings or to find an emotional source for our identity?

A partial answer may be discovered within the performance of historical drama. One of the results of staging such a performance is that the audience is caught up in the historical moment, recognizing and participating in a conjoint, national past.

Folklore in Use 2, 43–52 (1994)

Irish Stories Old and New: Community and Change in the Two Irelands

Clodagh Brennan Harvey

This presentation explores a number of aspects of traditional culture and their relationship—at the level of popular culture—to contemporary developments in the storytelling traditions of Ireland, Northern Ireland, and the United States. I conducted extensive field research on traditional storytelling in the Republic of Ireland and Northern Ireland in 1981 and 1983–1984. Two later trips to Northern Ireland in the early 1990s made it possible for me to do additional research and to assess the accuracy of some of my earlier predictions concerning the prognosis for Irish traditional storytelling in English and the possible impact on Irish tradition of the international storytelling revival.[1] I will make some tentative observations regarding developments in popular oral storytelling on both sides of the Atlantic and illustrate some ways in which a popular traditional Irish tale, "The Man Who Had No Story," has been reworked in performance for contemporary audiences. I will begin by highlighting briefly some of the findings of my earlier research, looking at the relative status of the two language traditions as I found them in the 1980s.

By the mid-1980s in Ireland storytelling in Gaelic was still prized as one of the "glories" of Irish traditional culture at the national level despite the continued erosion of Irish as the vernacular language of the *Gaeltacht* (Irish speaking) areas. This was accomplished in part by the existence of the *Oireachtas*, a yearly festival of Irish traditional arts which

---

[1]In 1990 I participated in a "Folklore Study Tour" to Northern Ireland involving ten American folklorists and museum specialists and sponsored by the British Council in Washington, DC. This made it possible for me to attend some of the sessions of the Ulster Storytelling Festival, an annual event held on the grounds of the Ulster Folk and Transport Museum since 1987. I returned to Northern Ireland for a six-month research attachment at the Ulster Folk and Transport Museum in January of 1993 to do additional research on contemporary storytelling.

provides a nationally-recognized forum in which traditional storytellers in Irish can display their linguistic skill and virtuosity. The aesthetic canons of storytelling in Irish are clearly defined by the *Oireachtas* adjudicators and are understood by the competitors. Many of the storytellers in Irish that I interviewed knew each other and had seen each other perform and were thus capable of evaluating individual performance styles and the regional differences they represented. Even more importantly, exponents of the Irish language tradition had also had the continued attention of Irish folklorists, folklore collectors, and literary scholars since the late 1920s when the systematic collecting of Irish folklore was first inaugurated under the auspices of the Irish government.

In contrast, the English language tradition and its exponents had clearly been marginalized. Almost all the narrators of traditional tales that I interviewed, particularly the tellers of long, structurally-complex tales, had become "passive bearers" of tradition. They rarely told stories in the traditional domestic or occupational contexts of the past and had few formal or informal opportunities to recount their tales; they frequently narrated only for folklore collectors, if at all. By and large they were unknown to each other and had no forum with the national prestige of the *Oireachtas* in which to perform. The storytelling tradition in English had essentially become a cultural backwater regardless of the status of English as the first language of the overwhelming majority of the population and the medium of a parallel and long-standing vernacular tradition.[2]

Things look quite different today. The growth in the popularity of oral storytelling internationally during the last two decades has produced some interesting changes in the Irish storytelling tradition in English, although these changes have gone in different directions in Northern Ireland and in the Republic, as we shall see. To begin with, American storytellers are travelling to Ireland and the British Isles generally to learn firsthand about the tales and the exponents of these traditions. When they return home to perform these stories in amateur or professional venues, their audiences become aware that traditional stories are still the possession of living storytellers and not merely the documentation of traditions and customs of the past. Secondly, the storytelling festivals that have been cropping up in cities around the world (including London, Belfast, and, more recently, Dublin) provide an inducement for interested individuals to respond to the challenge to become "storytellers" by their active participation in these festivals and those of a more local nature.

---

[2]See Harvey 1992 for the results of this research.

Since many of these new storytellers do not perceive themselves as coming from a particular "oral tradition," they frequently dip into the traditional narratives of many cultures—usually through published collections of folktales—for material to perform, thereby enhancing the "multicultural" ambience of the revival. Storytellers old and new, including Irish storytellers of the old persuasion, have become more aware that there is a growing interest in traditional tales outside the academic world and outside Ireland and that there are potential social and financial inducements to begin to tell again the old stories. In fact, a few "old timers" do occasionally take the risk of performing for contemporary audiences. Let us look at some examples of the infusion of the old into the new.

Three contemporary Irish storytellers represent interesting stages of proximity to the old storytelling tradition and involvement with the current storytelling revival. Francie Kennelly of Miltown Malbay, Co. Clare, has made the transition from "passive bearer" of tradition to a modern performer of "Irish tales." When I met Francie in 1983, he had had some of his stories recorded by the professional folklore collector, Tom Munnelly, who lives in Miltown. Tom was originally referred to Francie by a local schoolteacher who had become aware in casual conversation with Francie that he knew some of the "old tales." Francie's continued contact with Mr Munnelly provided the impetus for him to begin to work up these old stories, and he went on to tell some of them publicly at the Willie Clancy Summer School in Miltown and, later, at the International Storytelling Festival in London (1987). Here we have an individual who had never considered himself a storyteller prior to his contact with folklore collectors coming to represent the Irish storytelling tradition on an international stage.

John Campbell of Forkhill, Co. Armagh, is now probably Northern Ireland's premier storyteller and a traditional singer of some note. John's true metier is the telling of humorous tales about local events and characters, relying heavily on the use of local dialect, but he was also the youngest storyteller (b. 1933) I had met with any real command of the long and structurally-complex tales (*sean-sgéalta*). By the time of our meeting in 1983 John had been telling his stories regularly at the *Comhaltas Ceoltóirí Éireann* sessions in Forkhill for about ten years and had performed on radio and television and in numerous other live venues. Since then John has toured Canada and performed at the International Storytelling Festival in London, a performance which, being broadcast on the BBC World Service, reached an international audience of about 50 million people (1987). In the Fall of 1990 the British Council sponsored a performance/workshop tour of the East Coast of the United States showcasing John and well-known traditional singer from Northern

Ireland, Len Graham. Mr Campbell is a much-beloved personality in Northern Ireland and usually a featured performer at the Ulster Storytelling Festival. Both John and Francie Kennelly have brought their tales from the traditional work and social contexts of the past into the milieu of the international storytelling revival.

Clare storyteller, Eddie Lenihan, began storytelling publicly within the context of the revival and with a conscious commitment to the tradition-ality of his material. Originally from Brosna, Co. Kerry, Mr Lenihan now lives in Clare and teaches school in Limerick. He has published several well-researched books on Irish folklore and has had a storytelling programme for children on *Radio Telefís Éireann*. I first saw Eddie perform at the Ulster Storytelling Festival in 1990 and finally had an opportunity to interview him at some length in March (1993) in Ennis, Co. Clare. Eddie's performance style is highly entertaining, energetic, peripatetic and dramatic in the modern sense—in fact, quite unique—but his material always stands firmly within the storytelling tradition. He has performed in the United States on several occasions and in 1991 was a featured performer at the annual NAPPS Festival (National Association for the Preservation and Perpetuation of Storytelling) in Jonesboro, Tennessee. Since Eddie Lenihan performs a complex version of the popular Irish tale "The Man Who Had No Story" (AT 2412B, *The Types of the Irish Folktale*), a story which seems to embody many of the emotional impulses at work in the storytelling revival, we can examine several commercial reworkings of the narrative to illustrate possible transformations a tale may undergo in its journey from the printed page to modern performance contexts.

Most contemporary renderings of the tale on the eastern side of the Atlantic are influenced by the version which appears in Sean O'Sullivan's *Folktales of Ireland* (O'Sullivan 1966). O'Sullivan ascribes the tale to the category of "fantastic nightmarish adventures," pointing out that it was "generally told as a humorous tale" (1966:274) O'Sullivan and Christian-sen's *The Types of the Irish Folktale* provides this summary:

> A man gets lodgings at a house one night. After a meal, he is asked to tell a story or to sing a song. When he replies that he can do neither, he is asked to go outside on some errand, and for several hours he has fantastic experiences. When he returns to the house, exhausted, next morning and tells the people there about what he suffered, they tell him that he will always have that, as a story, to tell in the future. (Ó'Súilleabháin and Christiansen 1963:343).

The version published in *Folktales of Ireland*, recorded in the Cork *Gaeltacht* in 1933, is largely true to type: the protagonist, Rory O'Donog-hoe, set off for a fair at Macroom where he plans to sell stockings his wife has made. Night comes upon him before he reaches town so he stops at a local house for lodging. Rory joins the old couple in the house for supper as all its preparations are accomplished magically: "A wickerwork sieve filled itself with potatoes, threw them into the bucket, and washed them. The potatoes then rose up and went into a second pot." As the household settles in by the fire for the evening, the old man asks Rory to sing a song or tell a story. Rory protests he can do neither, so the old man chucks him out the door. Along the road Rory meets a man roasting a piece of meat on a spit which he is asked to watch. When the man has gone, the meat shouts at Rory: "Don't let my whiskers burn!" Frightened, Rory runs off, but the spit and the meat follow him, striking him fiercely on the back. Rory comes to a house he soon recognizes as the house from which he was earlier ejected. Asked to explain his cuts and bruises, he recounts his adventures since leaving the old couple, to which the man of the house replies, "If you had a story like that to tell me when I asked you, you wouldn't have been out till now." Rory stays the night, and when he wakes in the morning he finds himself on the roadside with no trace of house or dwelling anywhere (O'Sullivan 1966:182–4).

I first heard an American reworking of "The Man Who Had No Story" on a 1986 tape entitled "Milk From the Bull's Horn: Tales of Nurturing Men," a collection of stories by Doug Lipman (Lipman 1986). Doug is a well-known Boston storyteller who actually specializes in Jewish stories. The liner notes inform us that "Doug's highly adapted version most closely follows the one given in *Folktales of Ireland*," which served as its source. In Doug's reworking, the protagonist, still named Rory O'Donoghoe, is characterized as "slow at learning things," always making mistakes, constantly badgered by his wife and those around him. Eventually a neighbor teaches Rory how to knit stockings and, as Rory becomes more and more proficient, the demand for his stockings increases. Soon all the villagers have purchased Rory's stockings and he decides to establish a larger market for his goods. Against the predictable remonstrations of his friends and neighbors, Rory sets out for villages farther afield, for the first time in his life taking the road *away* from his own village.

From this point on Doug consistently and deliberately highlights the psychological aspects of the tale. Rory is not merely a figure who doesn't sing or tell stories; Rory does not *know* any songs because as a child he was inhibited from speaking and relating his own experiences. When Rory is chastised by the meat for not turning the spit, he does not run away out of fear, but—as part of his bid for independence—refuses to turn meat that talks back to him. Throughout Doug's rendition, a developmental and psychological subtext are brought into the manifest content of the tale. As a result, the major thrust of the tale becomes the achievement of maturity and male competence.

Another Boston storyteller, Sharon Kennedy, who has herself journeyed to Ireland to record traditional narratives, tells different versions of this tale for both adults and children. The children's version, "The Girl With No Story," is on a 1989 cassette entitled "The Turtle Who Wanted to Fly" (Kennedy 1989) In her tale Sharon consciously creates a highly imaginative landscape by employing elements of Irish traditional belief. The protagonist is a young girl, Siobhan, who, while out gathering weeds, disobeys her sister's injunction to avoid a certain fairy field. Once in the field, Siobhan hears beautiful fairy music coming from a mound. She peers inside the mound and, seeing a long dark tunnel, enters it and follows it a great distance. Finally, a light shining in the distance leads her to the cottage of an old couple, who invite her in. Inside, Siobhan recalls her sister's frequent warning not to eat fairy food if she is ever 'taken away' and passes up the supper they offer. When she is unable to relate a story, she is peevishly sent to fetch water at the well. At the pump Siobhan hears the fairy music again, and a great wind whirls her up in the air—north, south, east, and west. She returns to the ground unhurt and finds herself at a local festival. Here she competes in excellent form a series of tasks: playing the fiddle for a dance and curing an injured man by the power of her touch. Then, going off by herself, she is once more whirled about by the fairy wind to find herself at the old house again. Ultimately, she is praised for her account of her adventures, has a sound sleep, and wakes up in the fairy field to find that the whole village has been searching for her "seven days and seven nights."

Finally, Eddie Lenihan's version of "The Man Who Had No Story" is found on his fifth cassette recording, entitled simply "Eddie Lenihan: Storyteller 2" (Lenihan 1988). Eddie's version is elaborately detailed, rich in elements of traditional fairy lore, and complexly structured. As the story begins, the protagonist—Brian O'Connell, a basket maker from Brosna (Co. Kerry)—has taken to his bed because he does not want to walk the distance to *Poll na hErse*, an area associated with the fairies, to find sally rods for his baskets; Brian also has a strong tendency to drink away his own profits. As his wife threatens him with physical abuse by her brothers, he finally starts out. While cutting some rods, Brian becomes engulfed by 'fairy smoke' and has to make his way to a nearby house. Then follow the encounter with the old people, the ejection from the house, and the whisking away in a fairy wind (here explicitly called *sídhe gaiothe*, as attested in Irish tradition). From this point Eddie's version becomes much more complex and macabre than either Doug's or Sharon's. Brian returns to the house, but finds himself at a crowded wake. To counteract the dullness of the wake, Brian is pressed into service as a fine fiddler and praised for his "mighty music." When a priest is sent for, he is collared as "the finest priest in all County Kerry" and brings tears to the eyes of all with the beauty of his sermon. When it is found that one of the pallbearers is too tall, Brian is enlisted as "the finest surgeon in all Munster." With a hacksaw in one hand and a knife in the other, Brian graphically shortens the man's legs and re-attaches each foot. He then joins the pallbearers to form a "fine, respectable-looking funeral." Finding that the cemetery has no gate, the pallbearers must climb the wall, man upon man, till Brian is left to pull the coffin up behind him. As he is about to let it down on the other side, the *sídhe gaoithe* picks him up again and deposits him near the house of the old people. Brian relates his adventures and is told that his great tale guarantees a welcome at every house he enters. Brian spends the night in the house and wakes up in the morning in an open field with his rods and his implements all around him. He runs home, spends the next three weeks in bed, and never cuts another sally rod again.

Working with the same essential story core, the three performers have created narratives with important differences in tone, coloration, and message. Doug Lipman consciously reworked the tale into a story of coming of age: by taking chances Rory gains confidence in his abilities and achieves real adult status. Manipulating and working with her knowledge of fairy lore, Sharon Kennedy fashions a tale which manifests for children the bountiful potentiality of the things that can happen in the world of the imagination and the competence that *children* can achieve. The liner notes to Eddie Lenihan's story comment that although the tale "may appear an elaborate nothing, a large house ... without walls," it deals with simple but important truths:

> the importance of having a point of view on the world; the desirability of respect for certain places; the incompatibility of too much alcohol with family responsibility.

(Certainly universal—and not just Irish—themes). As these three renditions indicate, traditional narratives can consciously be made to function as a medium for highly varied personal and social messages which are meant to resonate in and for participants in particular performance contexts. When one returns to see if such elasticity is evident in the material being performed in contemporary contexts in Northern Ireland and the Republic of Ireland, some curious ironies are revealed (and some of my earlier speculations about the likely directions of popular storytelling are confirmed).

While contemporary storytelling in Northern Ireland is clearly a product of the momentum of the international storytelling revival, it is, at this stage at least, almost completely inward looking. Although storytellers from abroad are warmly welcomed in the north, local storytellers focus almost entirely on 'crack': short, humorous stories of a local nature, with jokes, puns, plays on words and use of dialect, and a considerable amount of material that would generally be considered within the realm of stand-up comedy, though of a far less aggressive or potentially offensive nature. There is also a very strong tradition of oral recitations, usually original material which then becomes popular with other performers. These are the subgenres which seem to conform to audience expectations in a 'yarn spinning' context, for I have heard traditional stories (at least longer tales) only occasionally at the performances I have attended. If anything, traditional tales, requiring the level and type of attentiveness that they do, constitute a rather abrupt change of gears in this milieu.

In the Republic of Ireland change has come very rapidly in terms of contemporary storytelling. At one Yarn Spinners session I attended in Cork City in 1993, the material performed was very much in the vein characteristic of Northern Ireland, focusing on local famous or infamous characters and Cork turns of phrase, but allowing greater leeway for sentiment and outright sentimentality. (The Cork session included the singing of well-known romantic songs with political implications, such as "The Fields of Athenry," which might have nationalist or 'Fenian' overtones for some individuals in Northern Ireland.[3]) But in Dublin, the inauguration of the Storytelling Festival three years ago has brought with it an infusion of the international dimensions of contemporary storytelling. So, while the activity of storytelling has had a longer period of germination in Northern Ireland, where it is well developed and organized, storytelling with an international flavor, and an appreciation of more 'exotic' stories and performing styles, has developed more quickly in the Republic, at least in and around the city of Dublin. Nonetheless, storytelling sessions in both countries generally seem to provide a form of entertainment that is self-styled and familiar, providing the participants with a link to local rather that international culture, and to their own past.

There is nothing inherently wrong with these developments except that the 'glories' of the Irish storytelling tradition that are constantly being extolled, and which are linked at the level of popular culture to the numinosity of the term *storytelling*, are little in evidence outside the ambience of Dublin. In fact, public awareness of the old narrative

---

[3]Political songs of this kind (associated with Irish political nationalism) would not usually be sung in mixed groups (Catholics and Protestants) in Northern Ireland.

tradition—its tremendous breadth and diversity—is negligible. As I have noted, American storytellers learn and perform myths and folktales derived from cultures all over the world regardless of the source of the material or the relationship of the individual storyteller to a particular culture or ethnic group. Irish storytellers are certainly capable of making meaningful choices regarding their own stories and traditions, but such choices are predicated on a certain level of knowledge and awareness and, indeed, an appreciation of a wider range of styles and material.[4]

So far, folklore as a discipline has chosen to remain on the sidelines. Although the Ulster Folk and Transport Museum hosts the annual Ulster Storytelling Festival, it is not otherwise actively involved either in disseminating information about traditional storytelling or encouraging participation in local storytelling groups. Professional folklorists in the Republic of Ireland, rather than providing some guidance or offering expertise to the budding storytelling groups, emphatically avoid involvement in contemporary storytelling because of the 'inautheticity' of the material and/or some perceived excesses of presentation. But the resurgence of interest in oral storytelling and the international momentum of the storytelling revival invite the participation of folklorists as perhaps *the* professionals with specific training in the area of traditional narrative; they surely belong in the arena. The growing awareness outside these islands of the richness of 'Celtic' traditions is attracting storytellers to Ireland, and to Northern Ireland especially, because of the inauguration of the storytelling festivals and the network of storytelling groups that is constantly growing. Furthermore, these developments, even on a small scale, have special significance for the future of Northern Ireland because a community is developing there across the sectarian divide around the activity of storytelling. The use of the Ulster Folk and Transport Museum as the venue for the Ulster Storytelling Festival provides an important neutral zone where individuals from the two communities come together to tell and hear their stories and to laugh at common foibles; such occasions are sadly rare in the north. The cities of Dublin and Belfast have become added links in the world-wide chain of communication that is the international storytelling community, and Irish folklorists generally—with their embarrassment of riches—need to take some responsibility for the ways in which their ancient storytelling tradition is presented to the rest of the world and to their own future generations.

---

[4]At the moment (August 1994) this situation is changing very rapidly and will be the subject of my future research.

REFERENCES

Harvey, Clodagh Brennan. 1992. *Contemporary Irish Traditional Narrative: The English Language Tradition*. Berkeley and Los Angeles: University of California Press, Folklore and Mythology Studies, Volume 35.

Kennedy, Sharon. 1989. "The Turtle Who Wanted to Fly". Arlington, MA. (Cassette)

Lenihan, Eddie. 1988. "Eddie Lenihan: Storyteller 2." Dublin: Claddagh Records Ltd. (Cassette)

Lipman, Doug. 1986. "Milk From the Bull's Horn: Tales of Nurturing Men." Cambridge, MA: Yellow Moon Press. (Cassette)

Ó'Súilleabháin, Seán and Reidar Th. Christiansen. 1963. *The Types of Irish Folktale*. Folklore Fellows Communication 188. Helsinki: SKS.

O'Sullivan, Sean, ed. 1966. *Folktales of Ireland*. Chicago: University of Chicago Press.

Folklore in Use 2, 53–58 (1994)

The Marketing of Tradition: A New Approach

Patricia Atkinson Wells

During the past few decades, we have witnessed a remarkable growth in the public presentation of traditional culture in North America, including community heritage days, celebrations of ethnic pride, exhibitions of regional arts, and festivals of all sizes. While many of these events are organized or sponsored by non-profit organizations, and are intended to be educational, the marketing of traditional art forms—including dance, music, foodways, and folk crafts—has also become big business. Professional fair and festival promoters, theme park owners, and tourism councils are in business to make money, and they do so by selling tradition(s), often not their own. This is also evident in the media of mass communication, which not only make esoteric culture readily available to "outsiders," but seem to have insatiable appetites for feature stories on lore, legend, and seasonal and regional custom.

Although the commercial use of traditional genres and motifs and the commodification of culture are by no means recent developments—it can be successfully argued that many traditional activities have always had an economic aspect—our present era of rapid social, political, economic and technological change has provoked a number of interesting cultural responses including movements to rediscover cultural traditions or redefine cultural identity, the growth of cultural and heritage tourism, "trans-ethnic folk romanticism" (Blaustein 1993:262)[1], and various official and grassroots conservation and preservationist movements.

What are the roles of the folklorist in the marketing of tradition? While some academicians might argue that, as scholars, our role is the documentation and study of these cultural processes and phenomena, the response of the public folklorist is more proactive. Driven by intellectual, economic, moral and/or ethical imperatives, contemporary public folklorists work directly and practically with individual artists and communi-

[1]Attributed to Barbara Kirshenblatt-Gimblett: "Voluntary or intentional ethnicity and participation in the expressive traditions of a given social or cultural group into which one was not born."

ties "to develop strategies for maintaining and creatively adapting their traditions to new social circumstances" (Baron and Spitzer 1992:3).

David Whisnant's perceptive examination of how "culture workers and other enthusiasts" perceived, manipulated and projected the traditional culture of mostly rural, uneducated and economically disadvantaged working people in Appalachia (Whisnant 1983) should be required reading for public folklorists. His chronicle of the actions taken by these culture workers in attempting to rescue and preserve traditional culture which they perceived as threatened by economic and social changes, including the influx of mass culture (phonograph and radio) can serve as a cautionary tale for those of us who are engaged in the representation and application of folk tradition. The "politics of culture," which he defines as "the interaction of disparate culture systems as systems" (Whisnant 1983:13) come into play when any "outsider," regardless of training and motivation, engages in "systematic cultural intervention." Whisnant defines and characterizes such intervention:

> Someone (or some institution) consciously and programmatically takes action within a culture with the intent of affecting it in some specific way that the intervener thinks desirable. The action taken can range from relatively passive (say, starting an archive or museum) to relatively active (like instituting a cultural revitalization effort). Its intent can be positive (as in a sensitive revitalization effort) or negative (as in the prohibition of ethnic customs, dress, or language). Moreover, a negative effect may follow from a positive intent, and vice versa (Whisnant 1983:13-14).

With this closing caveat let us examine some of the issues surrounding and concerns arising from "the marketing of tradition." What is meant by "marketing" and how are "traditions" marketed? As the word "market" comes from the Latin for both "trade" or "merchandise," we are looking at process (the verb form) and product (the noun). Going beyond simple exchange of money for goods or services, the marketing of tradition comprises such phenomena as:

- the transformation of tradition—modifying traditions to appeal to a perceived market, including changes in performance repertoire or style and the conscious creation of objects whose sole function is to be sold to tourists

- cultural appropriation—the use of traditional concepts, forms and symbols to create an association with traditional ideas and values, usually for commercial, political or ideological purposes

- "fakelore", folklorismus or pseudo-tradition—creating things that are *like* traditional things, also for commercial or ideological purposes

- cultural or heritage tourism—selling a community or region through its traditional culture, which may involve stimulating interest in a community or area by inviting outsiders to view traditional performance, the creation of traditional objects, and/or structures of architectural or historic importance, or to participate in indigenous customs or rituals.

What are the some of the problems or difficulties encountered by folk artists and performers in the marketing of tradition? One problem is that of public image. Traditional practitioners may be stereotyped as illiterate, backward, "simple folk" or romanticized as pre-industrial artisans or minstrels. As such, they are 'nonprofessional' in popular understanding. How can one make a living selling music or objects commercially— as a professional—when one's art form is supposedly a noncommercial amateur expression? (Rosenberg 1993:8) Another is lack of experience in the business aspects of selling or presenting their art. Almost every public folklorist can (and does) tell hair-raising tales of exploitative treatment of traditional artists by unscrupulous art dealers, collectors, promoters and/or producers. Many also relate cases in which individuals have lost much-needed social benefits because honoraria or awards (presented in an attempt to recognize their contributions to the perpetuation of tradition) temporarily inflated their incomes. It has also been reported that individuals who participated in public folk cultural programming have variously fallen afoul of the Internal Revenue Service, State Franchise Tax Boards, and the Immigration and Naturalization Service. It can be dangerous to engage in public displays of tradition! Other individuals may not wish to have any kind of public recognition for purely personal or religious reasons, yet they are ill equipped to deal with cultural or economic zealots who try to convince them that it is their duty to perform or exhibit to a wider audience.

What part can the culture worker—whether public folklorist, anthropologist, arts administrator, curator, or festival organizer, etc.—play in developing marketing strategies that will improve the economic condition of "the folk" and still preserve and protect traditional forms of expression (and their products and practitioners) from commercial exploitation? Among the diverse roles we assume as practitioners are those of:

- Advocate—serving as an artists' advocate within the community, a folk group's advocate within the larger community, or as a community advocate in a regional or political context ["The folklorist has the duty to speak as the advocate of the common man" (Lomax 1947:x)]

- Concert Producer—creating settings or contexts for performance and interaction; setting up staging so everyone is comfortable and the performer/demonstrator is not "on display" or intruded upon

- De facto Agent—booking performing acts and setting up tours or acting as an artists' representative to shops and galleries to help place art and craft objects

- Mediator—between outsiders and a particular culture group, between artist and audience, between traditional practitioner and the dominant "popular" culture

- Cultural Conservator—maintaining an environment in which local folk culture can thrive, enhancing a sense of community identity and ensuring the sensitive and respectful treatment of "living cultural resources", developing strategies for encouraging local heritage and folklife activities, creating programs through which heritage can be shared while the authenticity and perpetuation of tradition are ensured

- Tourism Facilitator—encouraging tourist visitation to natural community settings or contexts (such as local traditional or ethnic restaurants, the homes or studios of local craftspeople, and the local sites for music jam sessions) without alienating the indigenous population or invading their privacy

- Educator—providing the educational content and interpretive context for the presentation of aspects of culture or cultural performance

- Mentor or Trainer—providing technical assistance to folk artists and performers as an essential aspect of integrating folk artists into any marketing plan.

In 1993 the New York Folklore Society (NYFS) inaugurated the Mentoring Program for Folklife and the Traditional Arts, a technical assistance project. Made possible with funding by the Folk Arts Programs of the national Endowment for the Arts and the New York State council on the Arts, the Mentoring Program offers opportunities for technical assistance and professional growth to individuals and organizations engaged in or planning folklife or traditional arts programs in New York State. This includes, but is not limited to, folk artists, community organizations, folk cultural specialists, arts council, museums and historical societies. Highest priority is given to consultancies that directly benefit folk artists or community based organizations in ethnic, rural, or other underserved communities in the state. All projects are documented, and at appropriate periods following the consultancy, clients are interviewed regarding the long term impact of the consultancy.

How are mentoring and technical assistance "new approaches" to the marketing of tradition? Providing assistance and training in self-management and marketing enables artists to make their own decisions, to be involved and in control of their "career." This approach assumes that traditional artists and performers are intelligent, competent, and potentially able to articulate their needs. It also recognizes the rights and responsibilities of people to present and/or preserve their own traditions in the way or ways which best suit them. Marketing efforts instigated by the traditional or indigenous artist are likely to be culturally sensitive and may be predicated on considerations of cultural and aesthetic, as well as economic, survival.

Based on a decade of consulting in self-management and marketing for traditional folk artists and craftspersons, I designed a mentoring project for the NYFS in partnership with Daniel Franklin Ward of the Cultural Resources Council in Syracuse, New York. For this consultancy, I conducted an intensive two-day workshop with eight traditional artists and performers from Central New York on basic business and marketing skills. The training included information on setting up a business, keeping records, pricing work, sales and income taxes, self-promotion and the design of marketing pieces (including demo tapes, photographs, slides and videotapes), working with non-profit and public sector organizations, contracts and grants, resources for professional help and the importance of building networks of traditional artists and performers.

Each of the participating artists was already attempting to earn some portion of their income from a traditional art or craft. The immediate purpose of the project was to improve their management and promotional skills. Each artist/performer was asked to bring samples of any current promotional materials (such as business cards, brochures or flyers, portfolios, news clippings, photographs/slides and audio or video recordings). These were examined and critiqued and, where necessary, new materials were designed as part of the training exercises. During the course of the workshop, the participants produced resumes, personal or artistic statements and brief biographies. Promotional photography, portfolio composition and the elements of brochure design and layout were also discussed at some length.

In addition to the training, each participant received a draft copy of *A Handbook for Traditional Craftspeople and Performers in Central New York*, a substantial revision of *Handbook for Tennessee Folk Artists* (Wells 1989). The purpose of this booklet is to provide information which will help traditional artists and performers make informed choices regarding where, when, how, and for what compensation they will demonstrate, perform, and sell their art. It is my hope that the materials presented in the booklet and discussed in the workshop will allow those who so wish to take control of the public presentation of their traditions, and to receive their fair share of any forthcoming profits.

This self-management and marketing workshop/booklet package was a "pilot" project, documented and tracked by the Cultural Resources Council to provide feedback for the improvement of future consultancies for traditional artists. Based on the response to the first program, we expect that additional projects of this type will be developed in the state over the coming year.

One final result of this project is the establishment of a "coaching network" for the artists which allows them to ask for and receive assistance in self-management and promotion from the mentor/consultant, the Cultural Resources Council folklorist, other professionals, and each other. We hope that the preliminary success of this project will stimulate public folklorists in other states to institute similar programs.

APPRECIATION

I would like to thank Teri Brewer of the University of Glamorgan for organizing this excellent and informative conference, and for inviting me to participate in it. Thanks are also due to my partner in the pilot project, Daniel Franklin Ward of the Cultural Resources Council in Syracuse, NY.

REFERENCES

Baron, Robert and Nicholas R. Spitzer, eds. 1992. *Public Folklore*. Washington and London: Smithsonian Institution Press.

Blaustein, Richard. 1993. Rethinking Folk Revivalism. In Rosenberg, Neil V., ed. *Transforming Tradition*, pp. 258–274. Urbana and Chicago: University of Illinois Press.

Lomax. John A. and Alan Lomax, eds. 1947. *Folksong USA*. New York: Duell.

Rosenberg, Neil V., ed. 1993. *Transforming Tradition: Folk Music Revivals Examined*. Urbana and Chicago: University of Illinois Press.

Wells, Patricia Atkinson. 1989. *Handbook for Tennessee Folk Artists*. Nashville: Tennessee Arts Commission.

Whisnant, David. 1983. *All Things Native and Fine: The Politics of Culture in an American Region*. Chapel Hill: University of North Carolina Press.

Folklore in Use 2, 59–68 (1994)

Heroic Past: Some Perspectives on the Marketing of Folklore and History in the Middle East

GWENDOLYN LEICK

When I was at primary school in an Austrian village in the late 1950s, we were taught history, geography and the natural sciences through a close investigation of the locality, the very village and district we inhabited. The silver Sun-Chariot of Strettweg, one of the most outstanding works of early Celtic art, was discovered in a field just a few miles away. But there were also prehistoric vases, Roman grave-stones, as well as the ruin of a castle that had belonged to Ulrich von Liechtenstein, a troubadour famous for drinking his lady's bath-water. We knew which farms had been ravaged during the Thirty Years Wars and where Napoleon's officers had been lodged.

The point I am trying to make is not how rich this particular Styrian village was in history, but how strongly the teaching of history at that period stressed a cultural and historical continuity. School-children were made aware that they were part of a pattern of human lives lived in these very mountains and valleys for millennia. The tangible things left behind by Celts or Noricans, Romans, Slavs or Goths, medieval knights and poets, belonged to the area and belonged to us. The then still flourishing rural customs, the many folk traditions were also decidedly local, peculiar to the village or district. The consciousness fostered by such an upbringing was supra-national by reference to the past and parochially un-nationalistic by being within the folk-sphere of the village.

This personal experience of my early schooling is relevant to the general purpose of this paper that concerns itself with the Middle East when the socio-political background is taken into account. The then newly established Second Republic of Austria (1955) needed to develop a new kind of national identity. After the disasters of the Second World War as part of Großdeutschland, the notions of 'race' and 'nation' were over-loaded with significance. The question of what constitutes an Austrian could no longer officially be answered by reference to ethnicity, although the majority of the population continued to feel very strongly about the issue. Within its shrunken borders, the former empire reduced to an Alpine Republic, the question as to what is an Austrian became increasingly voiced in the context of the now significant tourist industry. Post-imperial, post-Anschluß, post-war Austria, could be marketed by stressing its regional historic and cultural continuity ("Forever Mozart..."). In the time of political and social readjustment, the notion of a national heritage, easily exploitable for commercial ends, also contributed to form individual and national self-consciousness. Incidentally, it also allowed for the pressing question of complicity in the excesses of the Third Reich to be shelved and repressed.

THE DEVELOPMENT OF NATIONALISM WITHIN THE OTTOMAN EMPIRE

After this preamble, I come to the main subject of this paper, the development of nationalism in some of the countries that were part of the Ottoman Empire, or close to it. The decline and final fragmentation of this vast realm was cataclysmic, the break-up of its politico-religious framework scattered peoples and nations, and in turn created peoples and nations. Like the Hapsburg Empire, the Ottoman state was multicultural, multi-lingual, with significant sections of the population adhering to different beliefs than the one upheld by the state. The great historical upheavals of the nineteenth and early twentieth centuries in both states urged an intensive search for cultural identity.

In Ottoman society the homeland was constituted by the boundaries reached through political expansion of the empire which comprised not only what we now call the Middle East, but also North Africa, as well as Greece and the Balkans with their Christian populations. The coherence of the protean empire however, was based on the Islamic religion. The Calif of the Golden Porte was the spiritual leader of all Muslims.

Contact with European states, especially post-revolution France, by intellectuals studying abroad, kindled an interest in nationalism as a political principle among Muslim peoples. The remarkable progress and development, the superior military and economic power of the West were first attributed to patriotism (Dawn 1993:381). Nationality was now connected with territoriality, and entirely new concept. Romanticism, as well as the works of Weber and Durkheim, had a great impact on the liberal Middle Eastern intelligentsia. The decline of the Ottoman state, so it was proposed, could only be halted by ascribing to Western ideas and by modernization, both fuelled by strong national pride. But what did that mean?

In Syria and Egypt for instance, there arose calls for an Arab national revival, first voiced by an Arab Christian Ibrahim al Yaziji. In 1868 he argued that if Arabs wanted to regain their 'rightful glory' they had to cast off the foreigner (i.e. Turk!) and rid themselves of bigotry (i.e. Ottoman Islam). Then the vigor of the Arab nations would reassert itself and the Arabs would resume their progress in civilization.

Turkish intellectuals on the other hand were much inspired by the 'Pan'-movements in Europe and Russia and ascribed to the notion of Pan-Turanism (Turan, an originally Persian word, denotes the area north of Iran and southern Russia which was regarded as the original homeland of the 'Turanian race', composed of Asian and European peoples, Mongolians and Aryans).

All these debates were primarily concerned with culture and did not yet manifest political claims for independence from the Ottoman state, but they did introduce, although tentatively, the idea of secularism. This in turn provoked a strong reaction from the religious establishment. The decline of the East was diagnosed as the result in the decline of true religion, and the remedy was a return to the 'pure Islam' of the period of Muslim expansion.

One attempt to meet the threat of disintegration posed by nationalist ideas and religious reaction was formulated during the mid-nineteenth century, a series of reforms known as *Tanzimat*. From then on, the supra-territorial, supra-national ideology within the Ottoman Empire was Ottomanism, which subsumed the corporate identities of religious and ethnic minorities and aimed at treating all subjects as equals, all defined as individuals sharing equally in the rights and duties of citizenship. This in itself was an 'enlightened' approach, influenced by European anxiety and actual interference on behalf of non-Muslim minorities within the Empire.

The different ideological perspectives concerning the state and the nation(s) became increasingly polarized and have determined the development of Middle Eastern states ever since. Secularism and nationalism based on the idea of the homeland on the one hand, and the fundamental claim of Islam for political, cultural and spiritual authority on the other hand, proved difficult to reconcile.

TURKEY

The first country to emerge from the ruin of the Ottoman Empire into a modern nation was Turkey. Mustafa Kemal Atatürk, its founder, defined the Turkish nation as being formed of those who make up the Turkish republic, who inhabit Anatolia and Thrace:

...who speak Turkish, are brought up with Turkish culture, share
Turkish ideals...these are called Turks, regardless of race or religion.

This strong cultural element of Atatürk's view of nationality betrays his
familiarity with Durkheim's works.

His major task was to make the Turks aware of their Turkishness,
which Ottomanism has submerged to such an extent that the very word
Turk had become derogatory. Although the Hamidian period and the
rule of Young Turks had seen efforts to foster a spirit of national pride
and the promotion of Turkish cultural renewal (by means of language
reforms, research into Turkish pre-Islamic history etc.) these had been
directed mainly at the educated classes. Atatürk however, went to great
lengths to convince the downtrodden peasants of their self-worth. The
famous phrase "Ne mutlu türküm diyene: what happiness to say I am a
Turk" epitomizes this effort. The official historical doctrine, as it
developed in the 1930s, and has been taught in schools ever since,
pointed to the early presence of the Turkish people in the Middle East,
and especially in Anatolia. (By courtesy of the Turanian race hypothesis
Sumerians and Hittites form part of the same ethnic group). His aim was
to have the Turks regard Anatolia as the unquestionable Turkish *vatan*
('fatherland') (Kushner 1977:101).

In view of Attatürk's commitment to modernization, and securaliza-
tion, he associated traditional norms and behavior, especially on the
countryside, with backwardness and superstition. He intended to replace
the social control of the city-quarter (*mahhale*) or the village with new
European laws and executive bodies. Traditionalism hence equalled
Islamic traditionalism, which in itself was incompatible with progress
and reform. Only in so far as folk-culture contributed to the expression
of Turkishness, as for instance in folk music and oral literature, was it
promoted. By the same token, the playing of Kurdish folk music was
repressed as soon as it was associated with separatist aims.

The present-day attitude towards history and tradition in Turkey
reflects the unresolved tension between secularism and Islam. The wealth
of antiquities attracts tourism and the marketing strategies make full use
of Turkey's historical treasure. Almost sixty years after Atatürk's death,
there is now indeed a strong sense of Anatolian Turkish nationhood.
Most of his reforms have been implemented and in spite of recent
political gains by the religious right, most of his objectives have been
achieved. When we look at the postcards that have been sold for the last
two years, we are struck by the number of images of traditional aspects
of Turkish life, of hay-making farmers, the bread-making women in their
kerchiefs. How are we to read them? As nostalgic images of a disappearing social reality? As a subtle reminder of traditional Turkish or indeed

Islamic values? As a proof that modern Turkey is now self-confident enough to flaunt its rural population's picturesque un-modernity?

The dichotomy between nationalism based on ethnic identity and secularism and the traditions of Islam that transcend and contradict such notions remains a moot point in the development of Middle Eastern states. The marketability of the pre-Islamic past and ethnic traditions often reveal the underlying tendencies.

For instance, if a regime or government espouses secularism and only harnesses Islam to legitimate claims to political hegemony, the pre-Islamic past may be exploited to boost the nation's self-image by focusing on past cultural and military achievements.

IRAN

An interesting case is Iran. When Reza Pahlevi seized power in 1926 he was keen to emulate the example of Turkey and westernize his country which at that time was not part of the Ottoman Empire. He introduced a series of radical reforms, carried forward by his son, the so-called 'white revolution'. However, while Atatürk based his republic on democratic principles, the Pahlevi dynasty eventually epitomized an absolutist monarchy, economically and politically dependent on the West.

One event illustrates the ruler's extraordinary vision of nationhood. It was the grand party given by the Shah at Persepolis in October 1971. The occasion was supposed to mark the 2500th anniversary of the original Persian Empire that Cyrus the Great founded in the 6th century BC (Shawcross 1989:38–48).

The Shah persuaded himself that he was the spiritual heir to Cyrus, that he too would extend and advance the Persian Empire. It was symptomatic of the absolutism and the isolation of the Shah from his subjects, that like some divine king, he alone personified the empire. He invited the world's leaders, as well as millionaires and film-stars to celebrated this pageant by the spruced-up ruins of Persepolis, that had been painstakingly excavated by German archaeologists for some thirty years. The world, if not his people, were to witness the apotheosis of his 'benevolent despotism'. The whole event was staged like a Cecil B. De Mille film—with the Iranian army as extras: their beards crimped like the Medes and Persians on the ancient reliefs, carrying fascimile shields, pennons and broad swords, augmented by the new women's contingents of the armed forces and the most modern aircraft flying in formation overhead.

Totally excluded from this interpretation of 'history' was the Islamic element. Ironically, the extravagance of this party, which cost some $300 million, with its catering from Paris (Maxim's) and the hairdressers from Carita, was denounced most fiercely by one Ayatollah Khomeini, then in exile in Paris. It also marked the beginning of the end of the Shah's rule.

Unlike Atatürk he never succeeded in creating a participatory model of independent nationalism. Four years later the revolution broke out and now Shi'ism was interpreted as the main vehicle for nationalism in Iran. The faith of Iran was to be her defence against the manipulative interest of the west and the encroachments of communism alike. It was also to form the basis of law and morality and thereby increase individual and national self-respect. In such a climate the archaeological schools operating in Iran are closed, the empire of Cyrus again an infidel interlude in history of Shi'ite Iran. Persepolis itself was heavily damaged in the Iran-Iraq war. Maybe this war, fought against a neighboring Muslim state with a significant Shi'ite population, has contributed more than anything to the strongly nationalistic claim of Iranian Islam.

IRAQ

This brings us to Iraq, much vaunted cradle of civilization. Saddam Hussein's Ba'thist government was officially dedicated to a secular, westernized program of reform and modernization, begun by the monarchy under king Faisal. Arab nationalism played an important part and ethnic minorities, such as the Assyrians and the Kurds, were harshly dealt with. Saddam Hussein also skillfully manipulated the religious heterogeneity of his country with its economically developed and predominantly Sunni North and the relatively underdeveloped Shi'ite South in order to unite his countrymen and demoralize the Iranian enemy.

His attitude to the pre-Islamic can be compared to that of the Shah. He maintains that the ancient inhabitants of Iraq, those builders of civilization, notably the Sumerians and Assyrians, were the forebears of the modern Iraqis, and that he, their leader was a new Hammurabi, a new Nebukadrezzar. This notion is best exemplified by the project to rebuild the Babylon of the Second Dynasty of Isin, the great metropolis, which like Persepolis, had been excavated by the Deutsche Orientgesellschaft since the 1890s. Though the real (in fact only the subterranean parts) of the famous glazed Ishtar-gate had been shipped to Berlin, he had an economy-size replica built in the ruins of Hilla, against a backdrop of a new reconstructed Babylon, with brand-new bricks, stamped, in the manner of those used in Nebukadrezzar's city, "rebuilt in the era of Saddam Hussein". But while Saddam Hussein's concept of heritage (*Turath*) may be as selective as that of the Shah, and as focused on his personality, unlike the Shah who became cut-off from his people to spin his fantasies in splendid isolation, Saddam Hussein promotes a popularist and highly consumable image of Iraqi identity (al-Khalil 1991:68–82). And in further contrast to the Shah, Saddam Hussein incorporates Islam in the range of his national iconography as the posters that show him as a Shi'ite (!) saintly martyr demonstrate.

Samir al-Khalil is highly dismissive of the plethora of public monuments throughout the country, but particularly in Baghdad, which he regards as symbolic markers of *ersatz* tradition, as for example the statues by Muhammed Ghani of figures familiar from the Arabian Nights, Shahrazade and Shariyar, Sinbad and Morgiana, or the bronze Hammurabi and a Gilgamesh next to a much bigger sculpture of Saddam Hussein. In al-Khalil's words, history, literature and a people's myth have become kitsch:

> ...it is revivalism of a sort that is neither creative nor rooted in a deep feeling for what is being revived. (1991:74)

But how can one evaluate the relative success of such measures; since primarily aesthetic and philosophical considerations leave out the social dimension, to what extent the Iraqi citizen is reassured, supported or even created by this intense image making, this marketing of tradition for apparently ideological goals in a country where until a few generations ago, the visual representation of living beings was idolatrous.

EGYPT

Egypt, too, attempted to steer a course between westernizing reform and the cultural and religious influence of Islam. Egypt of course has particularly spectacular pre-Islamic monuments, some of which like the pyramids that have always been visible. The pharaonic past, at first only exploited as an export of antiquities one would rather not have, was successfully marketed to attract tourism. The recent disturbances of so-called fundamentalist Islamic groups have targeted tourists. This signals not only hostility to western decadence which is seen to threaten the country, but also a rejection of a nationalism that would allow a historical, even cultural connection between pre-Islamic past and the present. But while archaeology and the display of pharonic artifacts are important in Egypt, they were intended primarily for outside consumption, the target was the tourist, not the modern Egyptian. This hesitation by successive rulers to imitate the late Shah, or indeed Saddam as Nebukadrezzar, by refraining from equating Egyptian identity with those of antiquity, may yet save the monuments and the republic.

ISRAEL

Finally, a brief look at Israel, the first Middle Eastern country I visited as a student of Oriental Studies in the mid-1970s. The state of Israel gave archaeology, especially 'my' period, the Bronze- and Iron-age, consider-able priority. Yadin, one-time minister of war, represented the dynamic Israeli archaeologist, whose excavations were expected to deliver scientific proof for the existence of the Biblical Hebrew state. Archaeology in Israel was, and continues to be, intensely political. The de-emphasis of the history of the Diaspora and the documentation of the holocaust contribute to the history of the Jewish nation which had ceased to be a 'nation' in the 1st century of our era. In fact the debate as how the modern state of Israel is to be defined in terms of ethnicity, religion and culture is far from finished (see McDowell 1993:643–662). The official representation of history and the marketing of tradition reflect the different aims. They can be seen as political in so far as they attempt to justify the existence of the state in the Middle East, but again, they attempt a re-interpretation of the past to develop the coherence of a highly diverse society. As in other Middle Eastern countries we see the conflict between a primarily religious definition of the nation, here the concept of Jewishness, and a secular one, which may include peoples of different faiths. In this respect the evaluation of the past based on continuity with a locality that was possible for post-war Austria or Anatolian Turkey, is in itself problematic and to find a solution to that will remain a task for future generations.

CONCLUSIONS

These brief impressions of some Middle Eastern states do not allow me to come to any general conclusions and indeed the complexities of historical developments of the area forbid simple answers. I have therefore picked out a few examples to point out some of the strategies adopted to create a common bond between the citizens of newly created states.

Cultural nationalism, secularism and political independence of nation states were the goal of Atatürk and many other political leaders were inspired by his model. In order to foster self-respect, pride and patrio-tism, the achievements of past civilizations were claimed to be pertinent to the present and indeed the future. In order to be successful the model needed to be centripetal, inward looking, anti-expansionist, and generally intolerant of minorities. The vision of the future determined by the vision of the past. Strong claims on a territory inhabited by a people for a long period of time stress the unbroken line of tradition with the past, even, as in the case of Israel, the occupation of the land was for many ages an ideal rather than a reality. In the case of Turkey the historical claims to Anatolia may be seen as fictitious by the western historians, but we are speaking here of the marketing of history which does include the creation of history, the re-telling of the past. If a modern leader is inspired by a folk hero or the 'real' ancient king, he forges and continues the myth that feeds his nation, or at least his present reign.

While we can often perceive a dichotomy between the claims of religion and the claims of the state, the one aiming for transcendence, the other for immanence, religion too becomes political or nationalistic at times, as in Iran and to some extent in Israel.

Islam, with its claims to subsume and transcend national identity has a stronger emotional and moral appeal, especially in smaller countries, or in times of economic crisis. The so-called fundamentalist movements are different responses to a variety of conditions and social unease.

But the need for a link with the past, for a regional cultural continuity that reaches backwards through time, is always strong when there has been a recent break of continuity. Modern Austria claims the Celts, Turkey the Hittites, Iraq the Babylonians...

And while a new king or president can glorify himself as the new Cyrus, the new Hammurabi, the tourist is baited with the illusion of stepping into the past. History, tradition, heritage—these terms are ceaselessly re-interpreted, re-adapted and filled with different meanings, as history itself unfolds.

POSTSCRIPT

The original paper was amply illustrated with slides which could not be reproduced for this issue.

REFERENCES

Al-Khalil, S. 1991. *The Monument. Art, Vulgarity and Responsibility in Iraq.* London: Andre Deutsch.

Dawn, C.E. 1993. From Ottomanism to Arabism. In *The Modern Middle East*, edited by A. Hourani, P.S. Khoury and M.C. Wilson. New York: I.B. Tauris & Co.

Kushner, D. 1977. *The Rise of Turkish Nationalism 1876–1908.* Guildford, London and Worcester: Frank Cass.

McDowell, D. 1993. Dilemmas of the Jewish State. In *The Modern Middle East*, edited by A. Hourani, P.S. Khoury and M.C. Wilson. New York: I.B. Tauris & Co.
Shawcross, W. 1989. *The Shah's Last Ride.* London: Chatto and Windus.

Folklore in Use 2, 69–78 (1994)

"This War Without an Enemy": A Personal View of Some Discontinuities in the Relationship between the Academic Community and the Developing Heritage Industry

Viv Loveday

Re-enactment societies are a fascinating phenomenon. They are composed of people who devote time, effort, ego, and not inconsiderable amounts of money to seceding from modern life and spending their leisure time pretending to live somewhen else. In 1993 there were twenty five member groups in The National Association of Re-enactment Societies, NARES, representing periods from The Dark Ages to the Second World War. Although diverse in their specific periods of historical interest these groups are uniformly based in acting out the warfare of their chosen period. At the 1993 AGM of NARES there was a group of *music* re-enactors represented but it was the *Military* Music Re-enactors Society, and even societies such as The Ermine Street Guard, who don't engage in fighting, *per se*, still do it in military uniform. Their public activities take the form of stylized performances of warfare or martial skills and equipment and this makes them keen to find suitable venues for their activities. Consequently, over the last twenty or so years, such groups have regularly been integral to, and often been the main attraction at, special events staged at heritage sites by both enterprising private owners and by national bodies such as English Heritage, which is an affiliate member of NARES. What re-enactors do, they do for the love of it, they are amateurs, but there is almost invariably a paying public for their displays and heritage businesses often profit from their association with re-enactment groups. The staging of such an event can cost many thousands of pounds, the performance is a saleable product and re-enactment groups are usually engaged because of their known expertise. In the area of 'hobby' re-enactment professionalism versus amateurism is a contextually based and often fluid issue when staging what, for the re-enactors themselves, are club meetings with a performance element, but for a sponsor, are heritage business deals.

This paper, using personal experiences of a long involvement originally as an active participant and later as a participant observer with a seventeenth-century re-enactment society, will consider some of the areas in which there is often friction between amateur re-enactment groups and the worlds of professional historians and heritage business-men whose territory they share.

My first visit to the University of Glamorgan was to take part in the 1978 students' Rag Parade, that quaint British custom in which students adopt fancy dress, often on a particular theme and parade through the streets of their town 'demanding money with menaces' or 'collecting money for local charities'—the definition depending on your feelings about the local student body. Since members of the New Model Army[1] habitually put on silly clothes to persuade the public to donate to charity, the students invited local members to take part in their Rag Parade and about a dozen of us duly paraded. It was a hot day and as we marched back to the campus we fell out at a local pub to have a drink. As it was lunch time, some of us went into a chip shop to get some lunch. The woman serving was a bit taken aback by the sudden appearance of half a dozen bodies in doublet and breeches, and asked us what we were dressed up as and what we were doing. This is meat and drink to a member of the Army, and I went into the standard spiel about "We're in the New Model Army and we refight English Civil War battles to raise money for charity and to show people what it was like in the seventeenth century," then, since we were tired and hungry, and hoping she might actually take our order, I added " and an army marches on its stomach, you know". At that moment an elderly man trudged through from the kitchen at the back of the shop carrying a basket of uncooked chips. He glared at me, declaring tersely, and with a strong Italian accent, "The Army of Cromwell marches on the blood and bones of good Catholic Irishmen" then dumped his chips in the boiling fat and walked out again. I was dumbstruck.

---

[1]"New Model Army" is a pseudonym and the names of participants have been changed to preserve privacy of individuals. The New Model Army Society is a limited company and educational charity, set up by a group of enthusiastic amateurs in 1968 to reenact battles and sieges of the English Civil Wars of 1642–1649 using seventeenth-century weaponry and wearing seventeenth-century costume. According to its Articles of Association, it aims to educate and entertain both its own members and the paying public who come to its displays and to raise public awareness of this important and formative period of British History. Its current membership is about six thousand and is one of the larges: re-enactment societies in Europe.

It is highly unusual to find a 'civilian' voicing any view on seven-teenth-century politics, and this incident was certainly an extremely formative influence on my subsequent studies on reenactment. I would have quite happily engaged him in a serious discussion on Cromwellian foreign policy in Ireland; but somehow I felt he had broken an invisible boundary, though it was some time before I realized how. The contrast between the reactions to us of man with the chips and the woman behind the counter could not have been more marked. Seventeenth-century reenactors are used to people not knowing about the Civil Wars, and even the most unskilled and historically naive member of such costumed organizations feels like an authority when faced with a member of the general public who couldn't tell the difference between King Charles and King Kong, and who is looking to them for 'expert' information. Even if many of them couldn't speak knowledgeably about seventeenth-century politics or social history, there are few re-enactors who can't sound as if they know what they are talking about when asked the usual simple questions like, "do you make your own costumes?" or "what sort of helmet is that?" People never rush up to re-enactors and ask searching questions about the minutiae of Laudian church reforms, and even those re-enactors who actively wish to disseminate information about the Civil War period, have, in some sense, to work their way out of re-enactment character and establish a civilian to civilian rapport. When re-enactors are self-consciously 're-enacting', i.e. when they are engaged in a staged performance, they are part of a private game where only they have access to the pitch, only they know the rules and only they know when they've scored a goal. Ironically the battle itself, the public spectacle, is the arena where they are least likely to perform for the crowd because their performance is essentially a private affair. Even though they may appear to 'ham it up' for the crowd they are actually involved in intra-group activities. The 'Errol Flynns' who show off spectacularly along the edge of the battlefield are not intent on entertaining the crowd but on creating stories of their exploits, for later use in storytelling and conversation which will mark them out as distinctively 'belonging', of *being* re-enactors because they have the right experience. Derring do is performed for the other performers with the intention of re-derring-doing it in private conversation around a campfire. These personal narratives are also performed in public, in pubs for example, where translated into re-enactment jargon with abstruse seventeenth-century commands, obscure and obsolete military ranks, peppered with nicknames and some terminology believed in re-enactment circles to be authentic seventeenth-century terms but which actually form part of a limited re-enactment folklanguage they will be virtually incomprehensible to outsiders; as in the following:

Squiff had this Berry by the apostles and he shook and he shook til this Berry's morion fell off then Grasshopper yells 'have a care' ... but it was ripple! So squiff's just getting up and this hedgehog fell on him [laughter].

Translation " Someone we all know by his nickname [Squiff] had this Scottish musketeer [Berry's—name of a Regiment] by the bandolier [(12) Apostles, twentieth-century slang, unknown origin] and he shook and he shook til this musketeer's helmet [Morion] fell off then an artillery officer we all know by nickname [Grasshopper] yells 'I'm just about to fire my cannon' [have a care]... but it was a very big cannon indeed! [Ripple—nickname of large artillery piece] So the aggressive chap who we all know by nickname [Squiff] is just getting up [after kneeling down to receive cannon fire as a safety procedure] and this hedgehog [a defensive formation of probably over a dozen pikemen standing in a circle and pointing their pikes (14–16' wooden thrusting spears) outwards to fend off cavalry horses, twentieth-century unknown origin] fell over him [laughter].

Re-enactment provides a (relatively) safe and socially sanctioned liminal space which is time out of time, and there is an expectation that the 'civilian' population will cooperate thereby sanctioning our alternate reality and respecting our performance space. When the man in the chip shop made his comment, he was making a direct contemporary political point. His comment was directly to us as real people in the here and now, and by doing this he refused to play the game of treating us in the same frame of reference as, Guisers, Morris Dancers, Mummers and other liminal characters. He also made it impossible for us to continue the game at that point. Although very memorable, it is a story I have rarely told and only in select company because it is too threatening to the illusion of liminality on which re-enactment depends.

There is within reenactment a hard core of 'Historical groupies', in which I would count myself, whose approach to the study of the history of the Civil Wars is closer to that of academic historians. From this group of re-enactment enthusiasts and the related and overlapping group with an interest in wargaming has developed a specialist market which both researches and publishes its findings.

One of these publications, an historical fanzine called *English Civil War Notes and Queries*,[2] was published by a librarian in Southend who was an historical re-enactor in his spare time. In the course of the first few months there was a running skirmish in its pages between one of the country's most reputable civil war historians and a well known young

---

[2]Available through Caliver Books, 816–818 London Road, Leigh-on-Sea, Essex.

amateur historian and re-enactment enthusiast. Through the course of the dispute a lot of the major issues involved in the thorny relationship between academics and 'enthusiasts' were aired. While ostensibly about a dry historical point, and the fact that the 'amateur' had challenged a professional interpretation regarding the Colonelcy of a Civil War regiment, it primarily revolved around reputations and hierarchies of expertise and drew in several other contributors, a Fellow of the Royal Historical Society, a Senior Lecturer in Social Psychology and the Keeper of a Major Civil War Heritage site but whose academic and professional credentials were never mentioned. Reenactment is proud of the fact that it attracts both 'Dukes and Dustmen' to its ranks but the essential problem with this aggressive egalitarianism is that when people hang up their twentieth-century persona and don their seventeenth-century costume you often can't tell the difference and even where there are potential benefits to be gained by accessing their civilian expertise reenactors show a marked disinclination to acknowledge their real identities and civilian qualifications.

In an open letter to the magazine, the professional historian forcefully put forward his opinion of amateurs operating in his field.

> Civil War re-enactment societies exist on the fringe of the mainstream of historical debate. They contain within them both campfollowers and enthusiastic amateurs and admittedly one or two first class young historians ... by their very nature they are not contributors to the process by which we understand the past which is the purpose of history they merely serve to fill out the details which are not in themselves important in our search for that understanding ... I do not write in this vein solely to criticise nor to play down your role within the milieu for which you cater ... I merely seek to remind you that there is a dividing line between what N & Q should be doing and what in academic terms is historically important. *The work of academics such as myself is clearly lacking in some dimension of the period* [my emphasis] and this encourages your readers and most of your contributors to make up this deficiency with their own research. But they really must apply themselves in a proper historical manner and not be sidetracked by minor matters into the vanity of always supposing themselves right.

The implication of this rebuke seems to be that in any disputed situation 'amateurs' should always suppose themselves to be wrong and I shall make no further comment on the matter of vanity. However, from the fairly small group of original enthusiasts who wrote for *ECWN&Q* several have gone on to positions within the Heritage Industry, including seventeenth-century sites, medieval sites, and the National Army museum, while other reenactors of a less literary bent have also turned their hobby into their profession in similar positions at sites such as the Worcester Commandery. Ironically challenges to the interpretations of academic military historians come from the same amateurs and 'enthusiasts' who are the market for their work. While sometimes an amateur's reputation can be built by dotting an 'I' or crossing a 'T' of the work of the professionals (some of whom actually rely on the unsung labors of enthusiasts in collecting data for them), modern technology such as Desktop Publishing is enabling niche marketing of short-run, limited interest, works on highly specific topics as never before and allowing amateurs to develop their own platforms for research. These amateurs are creating their own markets and spheres of influence in which they produce and disseminate their own research.

More interesting though is the tendency for heritage sites in the planning stages and their early days to rely on the expertise and unpaid labour of these research oriented reenactors and then to dispense with their services; to 'use' them and then to 'lose' them. A local example is Llancaiach Fawr Manor, a site with which I am personally familiar and which I am using purely for illustration, not accusation. The re-enactment input there is not obvious, because there are no credits on any of the static displays or in the guide book to indicate our contribution. Suffice it to say that the first time I personally visited the manor I was delivering New Model Army costumes and musical instruments for the house, and we had to negotiate our way in balancing on planks through what was essentially a building site.

Re-enactors lie uncomfortably between being seen as too 'knowledgeable', and therefore threatening, by the heritage industry, and yet at the same time suffer from the contradictory ascription of being 'amateur' and comprised of mere 'enthusiasts'. They are also often oblivious to economic pressures and financial constraints, since they re-enact for the love of it they can have great difficulty in appreciating the difference between what they can do working late into the night on the kitchen table and what is feasible in a commercial environment. They do however provide a cheap and available resource, and though they are not usually employed they are often a willing resource to exploit until trained staff can be employed, regularizing what is after all a business. In this they share a similar fate to professional historians who are employed as consultants, again in the initial stages, but rarely retained after the enterprise is established. Again taking Llancaiach Fawr as an illustration, the research which goes on there is in the hands of their first person interpreters who have one day a week off-duty to pursue their own researches into their own characters or develop relevant skills such as playing the lute. Skilled though they are, however, they are occasionally prone to delightful chronoclasms such as rubbing their fingers together in the modern gesture for paper money or using some of the inaccurate traditional truisms consecrated by academic historians, such as referring to the *New Model Army* and calling it *Cromwell's* Army, when the Lord General of the Parliament's army in 1645, the year it was formed and the year in which the household are supposedly living, was Sir Thomas Fairfax. [The use of the term New Model Army is itself problematic as the nearest strictly contemporary reference is to 'Parliament's New Moulded Army' in a London newsbook late that year.] This folk misnomer was endorsed in the work of the first major modern academic military historian of the Civil War, Sir Charles Firth, whose magnum opus was the inaccurately named *Cromwell's* Army, (1902), and is a regularization of traditional usage post-dating the Commonwealth period when recalcitrant children were threatened with 'Old Noll'. As is often the case an historian's mistake derived from folklore and customary use has now passed back into General Knowledge.

Ironically, although often presented, notionally, against a backdrop of some historic site what reenactment does is to present people, not places and it is interesting to note that despite the publicity handouts and press releases and the way that such events are marketed, 'The Battle of Piddlecome Hall', in reality, would rarely take place within sight of the actual house itself but would usually be hidden away in distant fields. Any connection between the reenactors' efforts and the surviving building is frequently reduced to off-duty reenactors, often dressed in their Sunday best civilian kit wandering round a heritage site as exotic tourists. Limited general knowledge of the Civil Wars leads to some odd manipulations of history when trying to drum up audiences for presentations. The most ubiquitous local example is The Battle of St Fagans, 1648. This was the major battle of the second Civil War, and the largest engagement of the Civil Wars in Wales and has been staged in the grounds of Cardiff Castle, at Tredegar House, twice in Cowbridge out in the vale of Glamorgan, at Dyffryn Gardens also in the Vale; but, remarkably, never at St Fagans itself. When I moved to Cardiff almost the first thing I did was to go to Amgueddfa Werin Cymru/The Welsh Folk Museum (part of the National Museum of Wales) at St Fagans and ask them where the battlefield was, only to receive blank stares and be asked "What battle of St Fagans?" But as any historian will tell you, times change, and it is not impossible nowadays occasionally to find re-enactors sitting around a roaring fire cooking girdle cakes in the kitchens or practicing their weapons skills and chatting to the visitors in third-person interpretation. Although Brigadier Frederick Willmot the founder of the New Model Army, pointed out that falling off a horse in full armor makes an impression on an audience like nothing else, and the primary aim of these societies *is* to produce mass spectacle, it is probably

in these intimate interactive settings that re-enactment is at its most
effective and re-enactors can use their costume as a resource to share
with the public rather than as the insurmountable barrier it often
constitutes in other situations. Brigadier Willmot also regularly and
plaintively said that "Authentic is not a seventeenth-century word for
scruffy" in a vain attempt to persuade the army to address its endemic
inability to tackle problems of scale and proportion in its displays, and
come to terms with its inherently theatrical nature. The tendency of these
military displays to dislocate their, admittedly sometimes spectacular,
action from its social and historical context in which it would have taken
place seems to justify the view of historian David Cannadine, put
forward by Robert Hewison, that

> "our actual knowledge and understanding of history is weakening at
> all levels, from the universities to the primary schools. At a time when
> the country is obsessed by the past we have a fading sense of
> continuity and change, which is being replaced by a fragmented and
> piecemeal idea of the past constructed out of costume dramas on
> television, reenactments of civil war battles where there are no
> casualties, sentimental evocations of social conflict where there are no
> losers and mendacious celebrations of events such as the Glorious
> Revolution, which was neither Glorious nor much of a revolution"
> (Hewison 1988)

A frequent statement which army re-enactors try to correct relates to
much more mundane matters than the politics of the period. "You must
be a Cavalier, you're wearing lace and feathers", surely one of the hoarier
old myths about the Civil Wars, that of the gorgeously dressed Cavalier,
in Sellars and Yeatman's famous phrase "wromantic but Wrong", and the
austere Roundhead, "repulsive but Right". It is also a misapprehension
which many members of the army are actively working to eradicate in
their face-to-face interactions with the public, despite the fact that this
Educational charity has, until recently, included the phrase 'the Society
of Cavaliers and Roundheads' in its official publications. However, the
frequency with which New Model Army folk are also asked whether
they are representing the Wars of The Roses, or even the American Civil
War, suggests that Cannadine is correct and that a large section of the
general public lacks any useful grasp of the context of our historical re-
enactments and literally cannot *picture* history, which does suggest that
the early introduction of a solid visual element showing the development
of clothing styles and accouterments could be helpful to later understanding. This may counteract the fragmented perception of history identified
by Cannadine, enabling a wider understanding of it as a process of both
continuity and change.

If it is true that the first casualty of war, even play acted war, is truth … then we are all the losers when the major selling points of our history are reduced to the titillating and revolting bits. This not only disenables the audience from empathizing, the great buzz word for the learning of History in the National Curriculum but encourages them to feel superior. It actually creates insurmountable barriers between modern people who arrived by car, literate people, technologically sophisticated people from a society whose technicians can recreate what they perceive as the smelly, and squalid lifeways of distant ancestors creating our very own exotic 'Other', a set of wild natives who are not likely to make representation through their governments for the return of their sacred artifacts, and who will not complain no matter how grossly their religious practice is profaned and turned into a sideshow. It is no longer open to modern museums to mount exhibits such as that of Saartjie Baartman—'The Hottentot Venus'—a woman who was displayed as a freak in life and with dehumanizing prurience continued on display as just a disembodied trunk, buttocks and genitalia, after her death. Unfortunately a lot of the material disseminated through first person interpretation and through the heritage industry in general is of exactly this type, the sort of things that make people go "Urgh…", if the job remit of the heritage industry is to make their materials memorable and attractive then that necessarily militates against a balanced representation. If the essence of History as a discipline is addressing continuity and change the heritage industry necessarily prioritizes change, few people would be attracted to displays where demonstrating 'continuity' was the main priority—without 'difference' there is nothing to show. One of the most memorable moments of exotic difference I can remember in a New Model Army context was a cameo scene which used to be performed close to the audience in which a badly wounded soldier was dragged from the battlefield on a small cart and who then had his leg sawn by a surgeon off to the accompaniment of appropriate screams and lashings of fake blood. The soldier in question was an amputee and this was his little moment of glory. It never failed to cause the horror and distress to the audience which it was designed to elicit, but, spectacular though it was, and effective, I feel compelled to ask, why? Why is this sort of display used, what is its function, is it education or voyeurism of the worst sort of Hollywood kind? Conversely, if this sort of traumatic scene does not attach to re-enactments of warfare *are* the performers guilty of glorifying war, as peace campaigners who have protested against battle re-enactments claim?

Against this sort of background the debates between amateur and professional historians seem vaguely irrelevant. Both have the potential to influence the presentation of history and yet, as they bicker amongst themselves, about the finer points of historical interpretation and hierarchies of authority that self same history is being highjacked by a Heritage Industry which is not averse to writing its own if it sells better. In the words of one freelance heritage manager:

> if you've got something to sell, then package it up and sell it, and what's history if you can't bend it a bit? (Peek 1988, cited in Hewison 1988)

I can never see a day when, for argument's sake, Christopher Hill will don doublet and breeches and repair to a living history site where, through his everyday seventeenth-century interactions, he will convey to you the Marxist analysis of "The Century of Revolution" to quote the title of his classic work. Which moves us on to not a conclusion but to an urgent question; since it is obviously not 'History' which is being presented by heritage sites and anything designated 'historical' is rapidly suffering the same definitional degradation, are we witnessing the beginning of the end of history?

As a postscript; in the same issue of *ECWN&Q* that 'the Colonelcy debate' started, I had a piece published about Cromwellian folklore. It was a wild story about King Charles joining a fenland secret society of which Cromwell was already a member, 'The Society of the Grey Goosefeather', and I floated it speculatively with a request for more folklore materials to be submitted in the hope of opening up a forum for both reenactment and Civil War related Folklore. The one reply it received was a rather heavy-handed putdown by "a historian and folklorist and amateur student of the civil wars" who, since I was apparently an amateur on all three counts, was definitely pulling rank on me. Suffice it to say in the ten years in which *ECWN&Q* has now been running there has never any further active mention of folklore in its pages though I'm still waiting, but more in hope than expectation.

REFERENCES

Hewison, R. 1988. Making History: Manufacturing Heritage. In *The Dodo Strikes Back*, ed. John Iddons. Strawberry Hill: St Mary's College.

Folklore in Use 2, 79–88 (1994)

Fieldwork as Reverse Information for Local Tradition

John W. Sheets

The fieldworker trained in anthropology once felt comfortable and confident with an ethos of 'objective science'; enter the 'other culture' through your informant(s), make observations and collect data about questions then-fashionable, then return 'Home' to analyze and publish your results for academic consumption and reward. By its constant self-examination, reflexive anthropology has forever changed this logical, positivist scenario. Fieldwork is a dialogue between subject and observer wherein each will feel the effects of the other's presence, in place, in word and in print, to degrees that will impact the most quantifiable of results. Fieldwork in Europe can create even more complexity due to the existence of historical documents, the potential for long-term contacts and the subjects' reading publications about themselves; they have the means to judge and incorporate this information in a variety of local, regional, and national contexts.[1]

By definition, fieldwork within a local culture will accumulate information about the history and traditions of that community in a manner often beyond the subjects' interests, ambitions and resources. Yet, such information when published may enter the self-definition of local people as their currency of image and boundary for the external world. In our time of advocacy and reflexivity, I propose that we consider the data from fieldwork as eventual 'reverse information' which flows back to its origin, an aspect of 'post-fieldwork fieldwork' in the sense of Anthony Cohen (Cohen 1992). Given a long duration of personal contacts and numerous re-visits, the fieldworker becomes a 'reverse informant' who has evolved from the 'Outsider' who asks questions to a 'Confidant(e)' who possesses information. I have undergone such a transformation during my eighteen years of research about the depopulation of the

[1]Research supported by the Wenner-Gren Foundation, Sigma Xi Society, National Geographic Society, National Endowment for the Humanities, and Central Missouri State University. I acknowledge the permission of the Registrar-General for Scotland to consult documents at New Register House, Edinburgh.

island of Colonsay, Inner Hebrides, Argyll, Scotland.

As a 26-year-old PhD candidate in June 1977, I arrived at Colonsay's Scalasaig Harbour on the 'old ferry boat' for the first of my five visits to the island; it was also my first trip outside North America. After surviving customs at Gatwick, a London taxi driver, the five-hour train from Euston to Glasgow, an early morning train to Oban, too much luggage, British Rail food with warm beer and jet-lag, I marvelled at how much water dominated the lives and land of these people; I was born and raised in the American Midwest where water usually means flood and destruction after the spring rains. With the advice and consent of the local doctor (and the doubts of my doctoral committee), my mission was to collect demographic and genealogical data through a household survey and thereby measure the parameters of genetic micro-evolution in a reduced population—then go to the island of Jura for an identical, comparative exercise. The doctor forewarned me of the natives' reticence so I spent the first week walking everywhere, and waving to everyone, transcribing gravestones and feeling like an out-of-place 'Yank' who missed home and baseball scores. Once I summoned the courage (through an islander who worked at the Hotel where I stayed), I approached the households at the harbour with my neatly typed and copied data sheets, complete with a consent form which a household participant must sign. To my surprise, they knew me as 'the doctor's friend' and answered the questions about marriage, birth, death, health and ancestry as best they could; the difficulty came when signing the consent form because it resembled a government document.

I spent the summer on Colonsay and Jura and left with more than enough information to complete my dissertation and find a job. I kept a daily diary, as I have for every day spent in Scotland these many years. My memories of that first summer still evoke images of scattered houses, many sheep, the crashing waves and a remote style of life that I adopted until my step-by-step return home shocked me back into the frantic pace of loud America. The islanders' memory of their family histories meant kindred and friends gone away for ever; the older people would often converse in Gaelic when they tried to remember, then (thankfully) switch to English for me. Colonsay had experienced a near 90% depopulation over 135 years of observation, from 979 people in 1841 to only 125 in 1977. The reasons for this decline were the same as elsewhere in the Highlands and the Islands—local products like beef and kelp undersold in continental markets, overpopulation of the island, and the Potato Famine in 1846. Vacant houses and the ruins of thatched stone huts litter the landscape of Colonsay in testimony to the steady exodus of its people. I wanted to know more about the process and details of a community's diminution.

With references from the doctor and the minister in both Colonsay and Jura, I received permission from New Register House in Edinburgh to transcribe the population records of the islands from the late eighteenth century to the present. I returned to Scotland in 1980 and lived in Edinburgh for most of the summer. It was quite a change from the Hebrides, as the islanders warned me three years earlier; after all, it is the 'City of the *Sassenach*' in Scotland. Near the end of the summer I returned to Colonsay (and to Jura). Much had changed in my life since 1977—marriage, job as an assistant professor, birth of our daughter, publication of the first article from my dissertation—and I was as nervous then as before. Would anyone remember me, did they care to re-acquaint, or should I even be there? And so much had changed in Colonsay. Some families had emigrated, the Hotel had new ownership, the children had grown and a few of the elders had died. Much like Professor Cohen's anxiety upon return to Whalsay in Shetland, my return to Colonsay in Argyll was "...a confrontation with one's own aging and the passage of time." I treated it as a social visit, to meet the people with whom I spent the most time in 1977 and to ask their opinions about further research into the community's past. I violated for them what was a local rule about many visitors to Colonsay—'They say they will, but they never do return.'

This time my visits to their homes seemed longer and more personal than in 1977. They teased me about leaving my wife and daughter in America, and believed me when I promised to return with my family. It was also during this first re-visit that I realized I possessed the first installment of historical information about Colonsay from Register House which is both confidential and complete in place of the local memories then alive in the community. The ramifications seemed complex, numerical and technical: I could fill in the gaps of oral genealogy and link the data into extensive networks, give the 'living demography' nearly two centuries of time depth, and ask genetic questions about family trends such as age and cause of death.

In 1980 I transcribed approximately half of the data available at Register House, enough to try preliminary calculations about Colonsay's historical demography and put some harsh quantities to the islanders' collective *memory of loss*. When populations shrink, they also age. In 1841 over 30% of Colonsay's residents were under the age of ten; in 1891, after the population went to 381, 22% of the people were children this young; in 1977 just 12 of the 125 residents were under the age of ten. Said another way, 1 in 3 islanders were under ten in 1841 while just 1 in 8 islanders were under ten in 1977. Young, fertile adults quickly left Colonsay and their emigrations reduced the number of potential mates for those remaining; in 1881 Colonsay registered only *nine* men in their twenties. The rates of marriage and birth plummeted during the last half of the nineteenth century (Sheets 1984). One native observed in 1887 that "a marriage is a rarer event than a Parliamentary election" (Mackinnon 1887). I communicated these results back to Colonsay where the numbers made an impression, especially when the community discussed with government bureaucrats the future of services to an isolated, depopulated island.

In my office I started to link incomplete genealogies from 1977 with the records in Register House. Colonsay's depopulation had increased its degree of kinship among the islanders because groups of relatives from the same village emigrated, leaving in place other kin groups.

I returned to Register House in 1984 to transcribe the twentieth century marriages, births and deaths. I held such familiarity with the past and present generations that I could recognize common ancestors of the islanders from individual records. Only then did I sense the intimacy and consequences of depopulation once it seized a community. For example, Colonsay lost sixteen men between the ages of 20 and 35 in World War I; a beautiful monument at the Harbour honors them. Still, it cannot convey the demographic subtraction of manpower from which the island never recovered.

Colonsay's first resident doctor arrived in 1897 and he recorded causes of death in clinical (sometimes tragic) detail. The islanders often lived into old age and their degree of kinship suggested shared patterns of morbidity. There was another, quite unsuspected result of depopulation. Between 1895 and 1960 Colonsay had a 5% rate of twin births, easily above the random rate of 1% in other populations. Like the patterns of morbidity, the prevalence of twins may be a characteristic of such a genealogy of extended kin. Remote consanguinity between spouses, late age at marriage for the mothers, and the presence of a doctor likely merged into this trend (Sheets 1986, 1994).

For the first time as a family, my wife, daughter, and I returned to Colonsay at the end of the 1984 summer. Our reception was nothing short of overwhelming, *not* because I returned as I predicted in 1980; it was our 5-year-old daughter, feted by an aging community with fewer and fewer children. I spent the afternoon with the doctor to share confidential medical information and to hear about people either dead or gone. It was then I knew my status had changed from 'Investigator' to 'Informant', a reversal of my role seven years earlier. For purposes of analysis, I had constructed a comprehensive genealogy of Colonsay which still organizes my research. I knew biological relations over the last eight generations of islanders way beyond anyone's memory and I felt enormous pressure and opportunity to use this information in some local, beneficial way.

To make a long story shorter, I will leap to 1988 when all three of us returned *again* to Colonsay. In the interval I had examined household membership from the six census schedules of 1841–1891 (Sheets and Kelly 1987). As the population declined so did the frequency of households with a focus of husband, wife, children and a relative or two. Like rural Ireland this century, more and more households were single adults or they consisted of unmarried kin, such as an elderly parent with adult children or aunts and uncles with nieces and nephews; these data resembled my results from the 1977 household survey. For the first time I studied a non-biological topic on Colonsay which required new sources to explain the results. At the Hotel pub one evening a 'leading citizen' of Colonsay, a man everyone knew and respected, asked me if I was aware of "the famous professor" from Colonsay, Donald Mackinnon, whose "story should be told".

I distinctly remembered a June day in 1977 when I sat in the cemetery on the west coast copying names and dates from gravestones. One of the stones near the entrance displayed a magnificent Celtic cross and under it read 'Donald Mackinnon 1839–1914, Chair of Celtic Languages at Edinburgh University.' I still remember my immediate reaction: How did a boy from this tiny island manage to achieve such academic fame? In 1984 I had copied his family information among my transcriptions of the Colonsay records and he had older twin sisters! Professor Mackinnon held the Chair of Celtic Languages at Edinburgh for 32 years, from 1882 to 1914, then retired to Colonsay just six months before his death on Christmas Day. A treasure lies in the Special Collections of the Library at Edinburgh University for there rests the Mckinnon Collection of his publications and manuscripts. A friend of ten years on Colonsay pointed me in the direction of what might prove to be the most fruitful, collaborative adventure of all.

Donald Mckinnon left Colonsay in 1857 for the church's teacher-training college in Edinburgh. From 1860 to 1863 he taught school at Lochinver in Sutherland then entered Edinburgh University as an arts student. He graduated with first class honours in Moral Philosophy in 1870. Eventually he became the clerk and treasurer of the first Edinburgh School Board and at the same time published a series of Gaelic essays about language and literature in a new journal, *An Gaidheal*. After some behind-the-scenes drama, he was elected to the Chair of Celtic Languages in December 1882, was appointed by Prime Minister William Gladstone to the Napier Commission in March 1883, and delivered his inaugural address on November 9th. As a leading Celtic intellectual in Victorian Scotland, Donald Mackinnon located and translated ancient Gaelic manuscripts, promoted bilingual education for Highland schools, attracted Highland students to university education through his curriculum in Celtic studies, and promoted his minority Gaelic culture to the majority British public. In every sense of the word, he was an early ethnic scholar who used multicultural methods in the academic profession. Throughout his life he maintained contact with family and friends in Colonsay. He made at least one trip 'home' each year and in the early 1890s obtained the tenancy of a farm in the north of Colonsay where he and his family lived during the summer. *He* was the Native Son who observed how rare a marriage had become in Colonsay in the 1880s.

The papers of Donald Mackinnon at Edinburgh University contain many references to his Colonsay heritage. As a child he learned "the Islayman is worse than the Devil" and "consumption was not only hereditary ... it was infectious (Mackinnon 1893, 1894). His earliest memory was the potato famine in 1846 and the consequent emigration of islanders. Late in his life he could recall for an Edinburgh audience in 1908 "emigration from his native parish upon a somewhat larger scale—friends, neighbours, relatives parting in this world forever. No one who has witnessed the heart-breaking scene is likely to forget it" (Mackinnon 1908). He knew the personal tragedy of hard times in Colonsay—when he was 12-years-old his father and twin sisters died within a year of one another. His first two Gaelic essays honoured and eulogized his patron and the laird of Colonsay, Duncan McNeill, Lord Colonsay. Mackinnon wrote a famous series of eighteen articles in 1887–1888 for the Edinburgh *Scotsman* titled "Place Names and Personal Names in Argyll." Nearly every article utilizes examples from Colonsay. He ended the series with pride and concern:

> The lonely island of Colonsay, which has furnished so many illustrations for these papers, presents...s marked, and in some respects a pleasing contrast to its neighbours ... [but] in this decade the outflow [of people] continues.

With the participation of Colonsay people, in 1990 I started to focus my research on the life and career of Donald Mackinnon. They have revived memories of him passed down by their ancestors, found photographs and papers, and taken a proactive role in the work. For my part, I have spent more time in the Mackinnon Collection at Edinburgh, introduced myself to the current Chair of Celtic Languages (in whose office hangs a huge photograph of Mackinnon), and located his only descendants in Dyfed, Wales (who prompted me to search for their extended family in Ontario, where Mackinnon's surviving sister and her family joined other Colonsay emigrants in 1862).

Donald Mackinnon witnessed, remembered and recorded the depopulation of his native island. He is my informant from the past whose words connect the extinct and the extant people of Colonsay. On a national scale, he used his position and his heritage to challenge the romantic images of Gaelic speakers; he simply would not abide the simplistic and erroneous marginalization of 'Celts' by other Britons. In 1912, and close to retirement, he published *A Descriptive Catalogue of Gaelic Manuscripts in the Advocates' Library, Edinburgh and Elsewhere in Scotland*, still a standard reference for these documents. Yet he suffered defeats here and there in his various campaigns. The Ordnance Survey declined his offer to help with the place names of Argyll! (Campbell 1950:104–105). Mackinnon would not let this go unnoticed. In his "Linguistic Aids" essay from the Argyll series he revealed that:

> The learning of the map-maker is sometimes more misleading than his carelessness or ignorance. In Colonsay, e.g., a word pronounced by the people *Mullaraich* ['shielding bluff'?], the officer of the Survey interprets, or gets interpreted, *Maol-larach*, 'bare site' or 'ruin', and he so writes it down, to the utter confusion of the person who trusts to the map alone.

Similarly, ironically, and posthumously, Mackinnon may be the historical test for Malcolm Chapman's latest exposition of the 'Celtic myth' (Chapman 1992; reviewed in Kidd 1993). The Celtic Professor's inaugural address is one point of entry into his labyrinth of scholarship that challenges Chapman's retrospective (Mackinnon 1883). Chapman contends "it is difficult to look at the ancient Celts directly" without a Romantic bias. Mackinnon would agree to some extent because

> the discussion of Celtic questions degenerated too frequently into an unseemly wrangle, where more feeling than learning was displayed by the partisans on either side.

But where Chapman (1950:251) says "there is no such thing as a Celt," Mackinnon (1883:9) reminds us, much like the Ordnance Survey,

> the records left by the people themselves, perfectly reliable, but peculiarly subject to misinterpretation on our part, consist of ...material remains ... language and literature ... popular tales and folklore ... as well as books and manuscripts.

The life and work of Donald Mackinnon, 'fisherboy' from Colonsay (McPhail 1972–1974:443), betray and contradict other statements by

Chapman about Celts.[2]

I returned to Colonsay in March 1993 for a three-day visit to see friends, to learn more about Donald Mackinnon, and to walk in the cemetery where more and more friends are buried. So many of Professor Cohen's observations apply to my latest trip:

> [...Colonsay] has become less like itself—the complaint of the aging...the more one knows a society, the more one is aware of how little one knows...time no more stands still for our informants than for the anthropologist...

Like him in Whalsay, I have strived since 1977 to "preserve, so far as possible, the authentic voices of the community" and Donald Mackinnon now speaks from the past just as the islanders speak in the present. They remember him as their legacy apart from other people and places in Scotland.

All of us reconstructing the life and times of 'the famous professor' anticipate the presentation, even the publication, of his biography to the British public and beyond. This now includes his extended family in Ontario who provided family documents about Mackinnon's grand-aunt who served the czars of Russia (Sheets 1993). The Canadians are re-establishing their contacts with Colonsay and sharing the stories of their emigrant ancestors. Donald Mackinnon still draws attention to Colonsay, as evidenced in a recent travel book (Newton 1990:188–190),[3] and will contribute to its future if this translates into tourism. He prescribed this

---

[2]"...a major problem in the study of minority 'ethnicity' [is] that most of those potentially involved do not appear in the argument, because they have no interest in it..." (Chapman 1992:234); "...the views and opinions of those who genuinely *inhabit* [emphasis original] the Celtic fringe, as residents or native speakers of a Celtic language, are ignored or dismissed with remarkable insouciance..." (1992:237); "...an account of 'Celtic centrality' would, in its own terms, be entirely unglamorous—it would be prosaic, matter of fact, dull, like an account of a day at the office..." (1992:291 n14). I provide these quotations because Chapman also believes "an account from the 'Celtic' side would be unequivocally welcome..." (1992:210)

[3]Newton perpetuates the rumor that Professor Mackinnon "referred to Gaelic as the language spoken in the Garden of Eden." He meant the *opposite* in his Inaugural Address:

> ...Questions of philology... were decided more by sentiment than by scholarship. ...The enthusiastic Gael... declared that his beloved Gaelic was the language of Eden... (Mackinnon 1883:15)

antidote to depopulation over a century ago:

> ...you live for days oblivious of the bustle and strife of the busy
> world...The lonely island is becoming yearly better appreciated as
> a health resort and retreat for a quiet holiday (Mackinnon 1887).

The people of Colonsay, past and present, give me 'grist for my
academic mill' and over the years this research has evolved into a
dialogue which combines our respective visions. I am not, and never will
be or should be, a member of their community. Yet, so much of my life
has intersected it in unplanned ways.[4] Like Mackinnon, I come from a
small farming community which lost almost 10% of its population over
the past decade. As an anthropologist, though, I wish to write an
'unwritten biography' to revive a man from the past for his community's
place in the future. Upon reflection, Donald Mackinnon's life has 'come
home' as more reverse information from my fieldwork.

REFERENCES

The Bailie, 24 October 1883, 23, 2.

Campbell, J.L. 1950. *Gaelic in Scottish Education and Life*. Saltire Society, W.
& AK Johnston Ltd.

Chapman, M. 1992. *The Celts: The Construction of a Myth*. St Martin's
Press, New York.

Cohen, A.P. 1992. Post-fieldwork fieldwork. *Journal of Anthropological
Research* 48, 339–354.

Kidd, Colin. 1993. Review of Chapman 1992. In *The Times Literary
Supplement* (16 July):13.

Mackinnon, D. 1883. University of Edinburgh, Celtic Chair, Inaugural
Address by Donald Mackinnon, 1883, Maclachlan & Stewart, Edin-
burgh, Mackinnon Collection C12(7), Special Collections, Edinburgh
University Library.

———. 1887. Lonely Colonsay. *The Scotsman* (23 August):6.

———. 1887–1888. Place Names and Personal Names in Argyll. XVIII.
Family Names... *The Scotsman*, November 1887–January 1888.

---

[4]Coincidence draws people together in unexplainable ways. Donald
Mackinnon's oldest sister was baptized on 28 August 1833 and his first child was
born on 28 August 1874; my daughter was born on 28 August 1979. My first
friend, informant, and confidant in Colonsay died on 18 January 1994; my father
died on 18 January 1993.

R.290a.40., National Library of Scotland, Edinburgh.

———. 1893. Gaelic Satire. Opening Lecture to the Celtic Class of 31 October 1893, Mackinnon Collection B1(24), Special Collections, Edinburgh University Library.

———. 1894. The Gaelic Medical Manuscripts and their Authors. Opening Lecture to the Celtic Class of 30 October 1894, Mackinnon Collection B1(38), Special Collections, Edinburgh University Library.

———. 1908. The Melancholy of the Gael. *Ceilidh* of 19 January 1908, Mackinnon Collection B1(7), Special Collections, Edinburgh University Library.

McPhail, I.M.M. 1972–1974. The Napier Commission. *Transactions of the Gaelic Society of Inverness* 48:435–472.

Newton, N. 1990. *Colonsay and Oronsay*. David & Charles, Newton Abbot and London.

Sheets, J.W. 1984. Economic and demographic consequences of population decline: Colonsay and Jura, 1841–1891. *Northern Scotland* 6, 13–32.

———. 1986. Depopulation and twin births in the Hebrides. *Biology and Society* 3, 118–124.

———. 1993. Miss Catherine Mackinnon's 'Russian Fortune.' *Scottish Studies* 31:88–100.

———. 1994. A triplet maternity in a reduced population with excessive twinning. *Journal of Biosocial Science* (in press).

——— and K.E. Kelly. 1987. Depopulation and household dynamics in Colonsay (Inner Hebrides). *International Journal of Sociology and Social Policy* 7, 103–111.

Folklore in Use 2, 89–101 (1994)

The Marketing of a Tradition: A Newfoundland Case Study

Gerald Thomas

When Emile Benoit died on September 2, 1992, at the age of seventy-nine, his death was given extensive media coverage. Widely acknowledged as Newfoundland's master fiddler, as a gifted composer in the folk idiom, as a virtuoso storyteller and, above all, as an outstanding entertainer, he was one of the leading lights of the Province's folk music revival. Not only did local media pay tribute to his life and achievements, but he was also given a lengthy obituary on the Canadian Broadcasting Corporation's prime time national news (4 September 1992), with film clips of the ceremony awarding him an honorary doctorate from Memorial University in 1988, and his performances with the outstanding Newfoundland folk group *Figgy Duff* in its visit that year to the prestigious New Orleans Jazz and Heritage Festival. His death was thus seen not only as a great loss to the Newfoundland cultural community, but also a loss to Canada as a whole.

Until the age of sixty-one, an age where most people are anticipating retirement, he was practically unknown outside the confines of his native Port-au-Port Peninsula. John Widdowson had recorded him in August 1964,[1] playing at a dance in Lourdes, a small town some seven or eight miles from his own community of Black Duck Brook, and then at a party in Black Duck Brook. Apart from Widdowson mentioning him to me, I also heard about Emile Benoit as soon as I began my research on the Peninsula in 1970. But it was only in 1974, however, that he became known to a much wider public. In that year he placed second in a Fiddler's Contest in Stephenville, a town of some ten thousand people forty miles from Black Duck Brook, just off the Peninsula; the winner's speech talked about Emile Benoit who, he claimed, would have won the contest had he only played the fiddle rather more than the clown. But word of the contest reached St John's where it was given a re-run, and

---

[1] MUNFLA C115/64-15 and C116/64-16, this latter recording made with Memorial linguist John Hewson.

this was the beginning of his illustrious career as a professional musician. On the strength of his performance in St John's he was invited to play at a festival concert in Ottawa in 1975, played at the Mariposa festival in 1976 and at a festival in Boston in 1977. In 1978 our paths finally crossed, with significant consequences for both of us.

This paper details the high points of Emile Benoit's career, with especial focus on my personal involvement in it. Since I did not begin to reflect in earnest on our relationship until his death was imminent, having been asked by his family to give the eulogy at his funeral,[2] I will restrict myself at first to chronicling the events and associated responsibilities which marked our fourteen-year-long friendship. I will postpone a preliminary analysis of the relationship to my concluding remarks, in which I will address one of the central themes of this conference, "The relationship between the academic community and the developing heritage industry." To the general and objective goal of this theme, I will bring the subjective and particular of my own experience.

As I noted earlier, I heard about Emile Benoit long before I met him; but between 1970 and 1977, my on-going fieldwork had been carried out in the villages of Cape St George and Mainland, and had not taken me along the then unpaved branch road from Lourdes to Black Duck Brook. Now every year since 1974 I had taken students enrolled in my course "Traditional Culture of French Newfoundlanders" on a five-day field trip to the Port-au-Port Peninsula, lodging them in homes at Cape St George and Mainland. In 1977, as luck would have it, one of my students, herself a native of Mainland, arranged to lodge one of my students at Emile Benoit's home in Black Duck Brook. As it was a good ten-hour drive from St John's to Black Duck Brook, and another forty minutes to Mainland, I did not accompany the student into the Benoit's home, and thus did not meet Emile Benoit. But on our return to St John's, the student who had boarded with him reported that she had collected a few folktales from him, and this tidbit of information I filed in my mind for future reference.

In March 1978, Emile Benoit came to St John's in order to appear on a short-lived television show hosted by well-known broadcaster Peter Gzowski, *Ninety Minutes Live*. Emile gave a characteristically lively performance, upstaging other guests, including another famous Newfoundland fiddler, at that time no better known than Emile, the late Rufus Guinchard. They met for the first time on Peter Gzowski's show.

---

[2] At the family's request, I gave the eulogy in English; it was translated and published (Thomas 1992) in *Le Gaboteur*, Newfoundland's only French-language newspaper, appearing fortnightly.

Emile was lodged in St John's with a total stranger with whom he was not overly comfortable; but he knew of me, contacted me, and I took him in for the short balance of his stay.

Later that same year, Emile and two other French Newfoundland musicians were invited to take part in the St John's Folk Festival, as it was then called, and as I had some peripheral connection with the local Folk Arts Council, and as my work was known to its executive, I was asked to lodge the three visitors. This was the real beginning of our relationship.

My duties were simple enough, ferrying Emile to and from the festival sites, to post-performance parties, providing him with breakfast, and the like. As our mornings were our own, I took the opportunity in getting to know him, to record him. Now I had completed my doctoral dissertation, on storytelling amongst French Newfoundlanders, the preceding year (Thomas 1977); the study had focused on what I termed the public and private narrative traditions, the former of which I had had to discuss without reference, however, to an acknowledged practitioner.

So after recording a wide sampling of Emile's fiddle tunes as well as biographical data, and recollecting that a year earlier a student of mine had collected folktales from him, I asked him if he could tell me any stories. The response far exceeded my expectations, to the point that the book I had expected to base on my dissertation became a book dominated by Emile Benoit who, for all practical purposes, was the public storyteller I had not been able to include in my dissertation. But the book was not to appear until 1983, and a lot of water was to flow under the bridge in the meantime.

I was by no means the only person interested in Emile Benoit at this point. Kelly Russell, in the early stages of his own development as a folk fiddler, had recently founded a record company, *Pigeon Inlet Productions*, and in 1979 brought out Emile's first record, *Emile's Dream*;[3] in the same year, Emile accompanied the group *Figgy Duff* to play in Toronto, and

---

[3]Pigeon Inlet Productions (St John's), PIP-732. Kelly Russell was a long-time admirer of Emile and his music, learning many of his tunes, as indeed did many traditional fiddlers in the revival context. There is an informative essay to be written on Emile's influence on younger (and indeed older) musicians; at least one sequence of his tunes was orchestrated by composer Peter Gardner and performed, with Kelly Russell as soloist, at one of the Newfoundland and Labrador Arts Council Awards evenings. Kelly Russell, along with Christina Smith, another devotee of Emile's music and an accomplished cellist as well as traditional fiddler, played some of Emile's music at the conclusion of his funeral service.

another engagement at the Mariposa Festival; but while in St John's, Emile chose to stay at my home, since we got on so well. In 1979, this included a two-week gig at the folk pub *Bridgett's*, in addition to the now annual presence at the Newfoundland and Labrador Folk Festival, as it was now named. Emile was more than happy to reciprocate for my help with as much of his time as I wanted—for recording, of course, but also to perform in my lectures at Memorial University, where other colleagues who appreciated what he had to offer also brought him into the classroom.

As Emile became more widely known, so too was the call for his performances on the increase. In addition to acting as his chauffeur and host, I found myself acting as go-between for Emile and the pubs and clubs which sought his services; at his request, I began negotiating his fees (though until I consulted other musicians, I was ignorant of the whole process), and eventually holding out for what was top dollar for local musicians of his style, in what was a very limited market. Our friendship grew stronger, for it was now expected that my annual field trip go to Black Duck Brook where I and my students were treated like royalty; Emile's home served as the central base both for my students' research and the considerable partying which was part and parcel of the field experience. Of course, I was still recording him myself, at every opportunity.

1980 marked the beginning of a period of intense activity for Emile and myself. In addition to continuing the by now routine round of responsibilities in St John's, throughout the year, I found myself more and more involved in negotiations with organizations outside the Province. there was a lengthy correspondence concerning Emile's participation in an Acadian music festival touring the four Atlantic Provinces; he was the sole Newfoundlander in the show, which he nonetheless stole on a regular basis. By now I was systematically keeping a record of all newspaper and other media reports I could lay my hands on; his success with the *Pistroli en Atlantique* is thus well documented.[4] A television appearance led to an invitation from the British Columbia Government Employees Association for him to play at their annual convention in Victoria, BC. The flurry of correspondence and telephone calls brought home to me the amount of time I was spending on his behalf, and how dependent on me he had become for his business dealings. But he was more than pleased with the trip to Victoria; it netted him $500 for a half-hour gig, with all his expenses covered in addition to

---

[4]See, for example, *L'Evangéline* (Moncton) of October 14, 1980, pp. 2, 5, 16 and 38; and the *Nova Scotia Tourism News*, May 1981.

his fee.

By 1981 I had become Emile's *de facto* manager. If potential employers did not know it and approached him directly, he would quickly point them in my direction: "Talk to Dr Gerald Thomas," he would say, for he enjoyed a degree of formality, "He's my manager." Emile never gave me any instructions, trusting me to look after his best interests, and his money. If he was playing locally, he would ask me to pick up his pay, cash it for him if it was in the form of a cheque, and would then pocket it without so much as a glance. I had made it clear to him quite early on that I neither wanted no expected payment for my services—my reward was in what I was learning from him—but when he came with me to buy groceries, as he sometimes did, he would often insist that I accept a few dollars towards his upkeep. He particularly insisted, on our not infrequent visits to the liquor store, that he contribute to our bar; he would give me forty dollars and say, "Here, get me a bottle of rum, and get one for yourself at the same time."

In this same period, I had been working intensively on the final version of my book, but was also involved with a pan-Canadian group of centres specializing in French culture; funded by the office of the Secretary of State for Culture, each member group was required to undertake a project that would highlight its work in a way that would appeal to a broad public. Believing I could kill two birds with one stone, I used my allocation to produce Emile's second record, *Ca Vient du Tchoeur/It Comes From the Heart*, thereby illustrating Franco-Newfoundland culture and promoting Emile's career. The technical production and marketing was in the hands of Kelly Russell, but I had overall direction; as a result, the record was unusual, for I insisted that each fiddle tune be preceded by the story, in English or his native French, which Emile habitually told to his audiences. The album was accompanied by a brochure containing the texts of stories and the musical transcriptions, with illustrated biographical notes and maps. I was able, at a modest fee, to enlist Newfoundland artist Gerald Squires whose portrait of Emile graced the album cover. Produced on a shoestring budget—$6000—the album quickly sold out, although Emile himself did not like it—there was too much talk on it and not enough music to his taste. But it is a valuable ethnographic document and now a collector's item.[5]

The work involved was enormous. I have a thick folder of correspondence with the Office of the Secretary of State, but it takes no account of

[5]Pigeon Inlet Productions PIP-7311. Produced for the Centre d'Études Franco-Terreneuviennes and the Regroupement de Centres d'Études et de Recherches en Civilisation Canadienne-Française.

the time spent negotiating with printers, photographers, other musicians, and the actual recording, made in my kitchen and living room. As an academic production, I assume it brought me only minimal credit, though it did bring me a great deal of satisfaction; and, more to the point, it certainly enhanced Emile's reputation.

1983 was significant for two reasons. In addition to the usual round of bar gigs, radio and television appearances, classroom performances and appearances in local schools, with the concomitant managerial duties, 1983 marked the four hundredth year of the formal taking of possession of Newfoundland by the British crown, and part of the celebrations included a folk festival of international dimensions, with performers brought in from Britain, Ireland, Norway, France and elsewhere. Emile was of course one of the local stars, and his meeting with two French performers was to set into motion the eventual fulfillment of one of his lifelong dreams—to go to France before he died.[6] But it was to take almost three years of detailed and tedious negotiations before it happened. The second event of note, more personal in nature, came in late 1983, when I took Emile, at my own expense, to Montreal for the launching of *Les Deux Traditions*; Emile played a few tunes in front of Jesuit fathers who had published the book.[7]

A novel festival was launched in 1984, the bi-annual *Sound Symposium*, an innovative and creative event launched by local musicians of all persuasions, offering as wide a range of sound experiences as could be imagined, including a symphony of ships' horns. Emile was invited to play and give workshops on his style of fiddling, and quickly became a fixture. He gave his last performance barely two months before he died.

Emile had caught the attention of film-makers as early as 1979, when he was one of the handful of 'folk artists' chosen to illustrate creativity across Canada. The film, echoing Emile's oft-quoted phrase, produced by CBC, was called *From the Heart: Canadian Folk Artists*. In 1985 I was contacted by Walt Disney Productions with a view to using Emile in a

---

[6]Husband-and-wife team 'Hélène et Jean-François' (Salmon, of Nantes, Brittany). They were so taken with Emile, whom they entertained on our trip to Nantes in 1987, that they subsequently used snippets of his music, and his name, in their own chansonnier-style recordings. A ten-day-long musical cruise down the Loire Valley which they undertook in May and June 1993 was entitled "Ca Vient du Tchoeur", in tribute to Emile.

[7]Later revised and translated as Thomas 1993. I also devoted one hour-long programme, and parts of others, in a thirteen-hour series on French Newfound-landers I wrote and narrated for the national network of Radio-Canada in 1983.

film called *Portraits of Canada*. The film, using the 'cinema in the round' technique, had been commissioned by Bell Canada for Expo 86, the Vancouver world exhibition of that year. Emile was the star of the latter half of the Newfoundland segment, my help towards which, in contract negotiations and hospitality towards the producer and directors, was rewarded with a cameo presence on film during Emile's scene.[8]

I was also involved in negotiations with the organizers of Quebec City's Summer Festival, at which Emile performed with his usual success, subsequently returning a few years later for a second stint. In 1985, Emile also accompanied *Figgy Duff* to play at the Toronto Harbourfront Festival; indeed, he was to become ever more involved with the group, which found in him both musical inspiration and a new dimension to their performances. And finally, John Huston, one of the assistant producers on the Walt Disney film, who normally lived in Halifax, was organizing a new folk festival at Lunenberg; knowing Emile by now, he was most anxious to have him participate, and offered generous terms. Emile went, with *Figgy Duff* unexpectedly in tow, was a success, and returned there a few years later. *Figgy Duff*'s desire to involve Emile in their activities led me to write letters of reference for the group when it applied for funds used towards Emile's participation in their activities.

In 1987, Emile and I were finally able to go to France to take part in a Festival International des Arts et Traditions populaires, in Nantes. The visit, set in motion in 1983, had eaten up huge quantities of time and energy, requiring negotiations with agencies of both the federal and provincial governments, the intervention of the Canadian Embassy in Paris, and three different sources of funding. For Emile went to perform, I went as his companion; though I was obliged, to justify my own expenses, to serve as a cultural resource person for the Canadian government while I was in France. Thus I was called upon to give a number of formal lectures and speeches, and numerous informal introductions of Emile to the public and the media. At one of the

---

[8]Other film activities involving Emile in whole or in part include *Emile Benoit, Fiddler*, and *Ca Vient du tchoeur: Emile Benoit, musicien et raconteur franco-terreneuvien*, two half-hour cameos produced by Fred Hollinghurst of MUN-ETV in 1980; *The Magic Fiddle*, a 1992 British TV4 production by *Flying Fox Films*, which Emile did not live to see; he was featured in the film in a segment juxtaposed to another featuring Sir Yehudi Menuhin. Nor did he live to see the film made by French scholar André Magord, the English version of which, entitled *From the Heart*, was released on video in 1994. there are other films in which Emile appeared of which I have no record; film makers were apt to appear at his door at the drop of a hat, and Emile always obliged.

lectures, I called upon Emile to illustrate my points about storytelling, which gave a special cachet to the event, even though neither Emile nor his French audiences truly understood each other's French.

Making use of Emile's talents in this way was, of course, a logical development, not only in the lecture theatre of the University, but in the more formal circumstances of a conference or colloquium. After another complex round of application writing, however, I was able to bring Emile with me to the 1988 University of Sheffield Conference on Traditional Humour, where he ably illustrated the points I had been trying to make about humour in his storytelling performances (Thomas 1988).[9] In addition, Emile performed in a folk club in London, meeting a new audience and new admirers.

By now, Emile's reputation was so widely appreciated in Newfoundland that it was with a minimum of effort that I was able to persuade Memorial University to award him an honorary doctorate, in which he took great delight. At the ceremony he was given a standing ovation, a rare sight indeed in the context of university convocations. Being addressed as "Doctor" was more of a pleasure for him than one might imagine; all his life he had wanted to be a doctor—of the medical variety, it is true—but he was proud enough of his title.

Rhetoric of a different kind was necessary to coax more money out of the Provincial Government to help *Figgy Duff* take Emile with them to the New Orleans Jazz and Heritage Festival. It was considered sufficiently important in St John's that a CBC film crew accompanied them, with a half-hour report on the local television news following their return.

Emile and I enjoyed one final major voyage together. In 1990, after the usual long-drawn-out negotiations with three levels of government, I was able to obtain enough monies to take Emile with me to the 4th meeting of the Société Internationale d'Ethnographie et de Folklore, held in Bergen, Norway. Inevitably, it was infinitely more difficult raising money for Emile than for myself—I was going to give an academic paper, but Emile was going chiefly to be part of that paper, rather than in his usual role as a performer. However, having developed his taste for jetsetting, he was more than eager to accept the long journey, which we again punctuated with a stop in London, where he again played with his

---

[9]The paper outlined the characteristic humourous aspects of Emile's performance of AT 313, *The Girl as Helper in the Hero's Flight*, noting some of the features which he seemed to have adapted to humourous ends as a consequence of his interaction with non-traditional audiences. Emile then performed the tale, illustrating my points and, as best as he was able, answering questions from the academic audience.

Croydon Irish colleagues. In Norway, he never failed to grasp the opportunity to give an impromptu performance, at formal and informal occasions. My most vivid memory is, however, of the late Bengt Holbek sitting hypnotized at Emile's feet in a cramped office in Bergen University's Folklore Department, as Emile gave a spellbinding rendering of AT 313 *The Girl as Helper in the Hero's Flight*.[10] Fortunately, I was able to make several hours of video recordings of our travels.

In 1991, Emile was diagnosed with cancer of the prostate and given eighteen months to live, which he not only accepted with apparent equanimity, but even incorporated into his public performances, as late as July, 1992. My penultimate role in his career was to help his local Member of the Provincial House of Assembly raise funds towards the production of his third and final recording, *Vive la Rose*, superlatively produced by Noel Dinn and Pamela Morgan of *Figgy Duff*, which appeared, together with a successful video much shown on the Much Music channel, while Emile was still able to appreciate it, a few weeks before he died.[11] My final effort on his behalf was to compose and deliver the eulogy at his funeral.[12]

I have given this lengthy, though incomplete account, of my relationship with Emile Benoit for a number of reasons. It details on the one hand the various imperceptible changes that occurred—how I began my dealings with him chiefly as an academic offering a helping hand to a visiting musician; how I profited from his availability to record him extensively as a folk informant, and draw academic profit from the work, through a book and several articles, a record, and papers at international meetings. As time passed by, however, my academic involvement

[10]In addition to published versions of Emile's rendering of the tale, MUN-ETV also made a video version of him telling it, before an audience of students, in 1982. As a measure of his consummate professionalism and artistic control, it is worth noting that after asking how much time he had to tell the story, *The Black Mountain* as he called it, and being told ninety minutes, he took, without benefit of clock or watch, precisely eighty-seven and a half to do it.

[11]*Emile Benoit: Vive la Rose*, ACD 9014 & ACC 49386, Denon Canada Inc., 1992. The recording was produced by Noel Dinn, the founder of *Figgy Duff*, and Pamela Morgan, long-time singer and musician with the group and great admirer of Emile and his music. Sadly, Noel Dinn, who had been such an enthusiastic supporter of Emile, died a little less than a year after Emile, of cancer.

[12]Emile's funeral service was held in the parish church at Lourdes, but he was buried in the family plot at the cemetery at Black Duck Brook. His son Gordon subsequently carved a fiddle in stone to serve as a headstone for his grave.

paradoxically lessened, in the sense that I spent less and less time recording him, taking notes and so on, and a good deal more time simply being with him, absorbing knowledge about him as a person, penetrating, though with no great awareness of it, deep into his inner self, learning his profoundest thoughts, his philosophy of life, his world view; doing so in a way not usually given to most fieldworkers. Developing, in other words, the kind of intuitive understanding of an informant that cannot come from a casual relationship but only from such a long-term and intimate relationship. My academic interest was left far behind as I got to know not only Emile but his whole family, and his family's relationship with their neighbours and, indeed, with the world at large.

On the other hand, my support of him as a musician, initially a casual, almost accidental involvement, gradually took on a far more complex role. From being a host and driver, I became his professional manager; I have stressed how much time and energy this role consumed, while fully aware that had I taken on the responsibility on a full-time basis, I could have been much more successful in promoting his interests; there could have been more records, more performances, more travel, more success, perhaps. But that is speculation.

Our relationship was a symbiotic one. I can only judge what Emile drew from it by what he and others said. I have a letter which he dictated and signed a month or so before his death, that was given to me at his wake. His praise of my help and support was lavish, and endorsed by his whole family. I know how much he enjoyed his success. He loved meeting, and entertaining people, he loved his performances, whether they were in bars, in concert halls, or before the camera. He was proud of his many awards, from his honorary degree to the Newfoundland and Labrador Arts Council's bestowal of its prestigious Lifetime Achievement Award in May, 1992; he was proud of the influence he exercised upon young musicians. He generously attributed much of his success to my efforts. By the time he died, he had become both a brother and a father to me, and I suffered all the emotions such a dual loss inevitable brought.

Just as my own preoccupations changed, so were changes brought upon Emile as a performer. Playing in non-traditional contexts, as his public career required, produced a variety of changes in his performance style, in the context of his performances and, I think, in the persona he chose more and more to present to his many publics. I outlined most of these changes or adaptations in a recent article in *Lore and Language* (Thomas 1991b), so they need not detain us here, though I will return briefly to the broad issue in my conclusion.[13]

I have refrained from stressing the phrase 'marketing of tradition' deliberately, because for the greatest part of our relationship, the notion only occasionally intruded. But intrude it did, in different ways. Producing his second record was a quite deliberate act of marketing, however modest in goal and achievement. I did not market my book on Franco-Newfoundland storytelling, in which Emile played such an important part; for me, that was a means of repaying French Newfoundlanders for their generosity.[14] The various folk groups, such as *Figgy Duff*, the many folk festivals and other interested parties, certainly used Emile's reputation, quite legitimately, I think, as a drawing card. My involvement as an academic was as a reasonably competent facilitator; I left to others the moulding of him to their specific goals.

Yet even here I was instrumental, in a small way, in helping modify his public performances. Early on he acquired the reputation of being a performer who, once let loose on the stage, gave little thought to the constraints of time or even of the as they were dictated by organizers. I used my influence to remedy this trait, suggesting modifications to a performance which might enhance it, based on my reading of his audience—especially important when he performed in France and was unhappy at times with his inability to speak metropolitan French. Emile generally accepted my suggestions, and did his best to incorporate them in his performance.

This of course raises a final question, that of authenticity. It is a question of concern to some folklorists, though not one that dominated my thinking. In new contexts, he had to modify his performance to suit new audiences. But his informal and direct manner, his materials, and his delivery, remained those that had characterized his performances at home. My role was perhaps more that of presenter—presenting Emile, stressing what his usual performance contexts were, dispelling some of the grosser misconceptions about Newfoundland, its folklore, or indeed about folklore itself.

[13]Other writings dealing in whole or in part with Emile include Thomas 1981a,b, 1985, 1991a. The only creative studies of Emile's musical talents are Quigley 1987, 1988.

[14]Another important aim, which I note in the Introduction to both French and English editions of the book, was to contribute to the process of revaluing by the Newfoundland French of their language and culture, a goal which has been more important to me personally in my work on Emile's recordings, films and videos in which I have been involved as a consultant for some fifteen years.

Gerald Thomas

To conclude, my involvement as an academic in the promotion of Emile Benoit entailed a major commitment—not only of time and energy, but of emotion. Yet I believe that the folklorist who, as I have done, stresses work in the field as well as work in the library, who aspires to become, in Herbert Halpert's words, a "compleat folklorist",[15] has to make such a commitment. Fieldwork means working with real people, and it is, I suppose, a truism that the longer one works with a person, the closer one grows to that person. But the costs are far outweighed by the benefits, both personal and academic, that are likely, in hindsight, to derive from such a relationship.

REFERENCES

Halpert, Herbert. 1979. Vance Randolph, The Compleat Folklorist. Reprinted for private circulation from Cochran, Robert and Michael Luster, *For Love And For Money, The Writings of Vance Randolph: An Annotated Bibliography*, pp. 5–17. Batesville: Arkansas College Folklore Archive Publications.

Thomas, Gerald. 1977. *Stories, Storytelling and Storytellers in Newfoundland's French Tradition: A Study of the Narrative Art of Four French Newfoundlanders.* PhD dissertation, Memorial University of Newfoundland.

———. 1981a. Contemporary Traditional Music in Newfoundland, *Bulletin, Canadian Folk Music Society* 15(3):3–6.

———. 1981b. Emile Joseph Benoit. In *Encyclopedia of Newfoundland and Labrador*, Vol. I, ed. J.R. Smallwood, p. 178. St John's: Newfoundland Book Publishers.

———. 1983. *Les Deux Traditions.* Montréal: Les Editions Bellarmin.

———. 1985. Emile Benoit, Franco-Newfoundland Storyteller: Individual and Ethnic Identity. In *Papers of the 8th ISFNR Congress, 1984*, Vol. IV, ed. Reimund Kvideland and Torunn Selberg, Bergen, 1985, pp. 287–298.

———. 1988. The Märchen as a Vehicle of Humour: Emile Benoit's Version of AT 313, *The Girl as Helper in the Hero's Flight.* Presented at the 1988 University of Sheffield Conference on Traditional Humour.

[15]Halpert 1979. Halpert's obituary of Vance Randolph, a long-time friend, stressed the degree to which Randolph had devoted his career to the culture of a single region. It is not of course common for folklorists to confine themselves in this way.

————. 1991b. Modernity in Contemporary Märchen: Some Newfoundland Examples. *Lore and Language* 10:59–66.

————. 1991a. The Aesthetics of Märchen Narration in Franco-Newfoundland Tradition, *Lore and Language* 10(2):39–47.

————. 1992. Gerald Thomas: Tcheques paroles sus Emile. *Le Gaboteur*
8(21) (September 18):4–5.

————. 1993. *The Two Traditions: The Art of Storytelling Amongst French
Newfoundlanders.* St John's: Breakwater Books. [Revision and translation
by the author of Thomas 1983].

Quigley, Colin. 1987. *Creative Processes in Musical Composition: French
Newfoundland Fiddler Emile Benoit,* PhD dissertation, University of
California, Los Angeles.

————. 1988. A French Canadian Fiddler's Musical Worldview: The
Violin is 'Master of the World'. In *Selected Reports in Ethnomusicology*
Vol. 7, ed. James Porter and Ali Jihad Racy, pp. 99–122. Los Angeles:
Department of Ethnomusicology, UCLA.

Folklore in Use 2, 103–113 (1994)

Selling the Emperor's New Clothes: Fay Weldon as Contemporary Folklorist

Pauline Young

The Oxford English Dictionary offers a general definition of the word tradition as:

>...that which is handed down; a statement or belief, or practice transmitted (especially orally) from one generation to another.

The same dictionary includes a further definition and you will forgive me if I select this since it most nearly conforms to the areas of interest raised in this paper. This is a late sixteenth century usage of the word to suggest "a long established custom, or method of procedure having almost the force of law". At least some of those "customs" include traditions which symbolically constrain and denigrate women. Wise women and witches, for example, feared for their subversive potential, are still controlled, contained, killed in contemporary popular culture by handsome male heroes brandishing righteous swords, and that cultural shorthand suggests a perpetuation of oppressive myths which celebrate patriarchal power. Much contemporary women's writing, however, challenges and reaches out to extend the boundaries of western patriarchally-defined cultural orders and traditions and "myths can be deconstructed and denounced, or re-written and reclaimed." (Wisker 1994:104). Women with powers which would have been denounced as irrational—and even perhaps as madness, can be re-assimilated into a different cultural order which acknowledges and even celebrates those powers.

The reappropriation of tradition, of myths, the re-writing and re-ordering of the magical and the celebration of the supernatural are all characteristics of the contemporary female writer, only the fictive methods vary. Contemporary fiction writers like Weldon frequently begin with the factual social and recognizably historical world and then juxtapose it with the fantastic, spiritual and magical. The inscribed cultural values of the one are thus informed and modified by the proximity of the other, so that the powers of the magical have equal consideration with those of the everyday. Weldon's work is full of such magic/domestic confrontations which re-position both the wise-woman narrator and the female characters in the text, so that everyday domestic 'powerlessness' becomes transformed through the writing/reading process and also within the narrative itself into an exhilarating potency.

Fay Weldon is today a well-known novelist, screen-writer and critic whose work is translated and retailed all over the world. Born in England, and raised in a family of women in New Zealand, she began her career as a copy-writer in the world of advertizing, where she coined the popular sixties slogan "Go to work on an egg." Before her prolific and very successful career in fiction, Weldon therefore had a solid and useful grounding in the world of the market where selling techniques were being developed which would fuel the consumer boom of the sixties and seventies. Her novels in particular read and respond to her largely female audience's conscious and unconscious requirements, and testify to her astute merchandizing abilities.

Thematically, much of Weldon's work is concerned with contemporary cultural marketing of the romance narrative—and more especially with its practical effect on women's lives. Women are investors in, and consumers of large numbers of romance, from media narratives (film, television, popular music), to magazines and Mills and Boon-type fiction. This is a very powerful industry and also a huge productivity growth area which begins with the gendering of children's toys and ends with the happy-ever-after page at the conclusion of romantic fiction. Culturally, and socially, women too often remain products of a male gaze; surrounded by images of the perfect woman who is aged between 18–25, a neat size 10, exquisitely formed and competent in the female roles of mistress, wife and mother, the 'ideal' construction of flawless femininity is promoted throughout contemporary western culture. Weldon sets out to deconstruct this image, to 'debunk' the fairy-tale romance narrative in a number of her texts, but perhaps nowhere so deliberately as in *Life and Loves of a She-Devil*. The novel's protagonist is a woman called Ruth who is the antithesis of the immaculate woman of the 'Beauty Myth', being large, clumsy, and physically unappealing. Her mother refers to her as an 'Ugly Duckling' and her husband, who has inculcated in Ruth a disproportionate thankfulness for his name and her married status, tells her that she is "a bad mother, a worse wife and a dreadful cook. In fact I don't think you are a woman at all" (p. 41). Her rival, Mary Fisher, who boosts the market in romance as a successful writer of Mills and Boon-type fiction, lives like the perfect princess in a fairy-tale tower by the sea, and is "small and pretty and delicately formed." Weldon informs us that even when distressed she produces "neat tears"! (p. 8). Most importantly she has the status and recognition accorded the proper incarnation of the feminine ideal. In contrast, Ruth has no self-worth and no sense of identity—since that identity is formed and framed by men and the man in her life has proclaimed her a 'non-woman'! Provoked by despair and a desire which is the appetite of despair she becomes the 'She-Devil' of her husband's taunts; as a 'non-woman', relieved of all normal female responsibilities, Ruth seeks power to alter and reconstruct—not society, nor her culture, for she understands that change at that level is impossible, but herself in order to exact revenge on her faithless husband and the values system which he serves and perpetuates. She uses her intelligence and her many skills to destroy her husband's business and to get him wrongfully convicted for fraud, to ruin Mary Fisher, and to achieve great wealth. In a bizarre parody of *The Little Mermaid* and *Cinderella*, Ruth undergoes painful and radical surgery, until she is, in appearance, a duplicate of her rival. The costs of her physical transformation and her transgressions of cultural mythology are very high. She lives in constant pain, and she discovers that although she has everything Mary Fisher once had, including fame as a romantic novelist, "she is not so special" after all; rather that:

> ...the issue of female politics rests with power: it is not a matter of male or female after all: it never was, merely of power. I have all, and he [her husband, now her slave] has none. As I was, so he is now (p. 256).

Two things in particular interest me about this cautionary tale; one is that it takes and uses traditional fairy tales and subverts them—Cinderella's ugly sisters mutilated themselves in order that the coveted glass slipper (bringing with it the prince/marriage/happy-ever-after package) should fit. The little mermaid was happy to endure silence and severe pain for her indifferent Prince (Ruth dances with her Pygmalion surgeon at a ball and "with every step it was as if she trod on knives" (p. 254)). The nature of the 'bargain' made in these tales is severely challenged in this contemporary text.

Weldon also intersects the Frankenstein and Pygmalion stories here, as Ruth, having been apparently made in the likeness of the under-valued monster re-creates her physical self with the help of modern science and medicine, literally 'killing' her monstrous body in order to create an acceptable corporeal female shape while developing a monstrously assertive ego. Unfortunately, in line with the Pygmalion myth, Ruth becomes that artistic object created by the male artist as an image of his own desire. Yet while the outward vessel seems to indicate a meek submissive containment, the assertive ego within it has been the very instrument of that change.

Apart from Weldon's borrowings and re-writings of traditional tales, there is the question of the magic in this text. It was interesting to see in the recent British television adaptation of *Lives and Loves* the producers read the character of Ruth very much as a creature with supernatural powers, giving her, at times of momentous decision, glow-in-the-dark Spielberg eyes as a very dramatic and supernatural special effect. The suggestion of an unearthly 'witch-like' power source which comes to Ruth's aid in times of crisis places her character outside the frame of ordinary female experience, thereby constraining and diminishing her achievements. Yet here, as in a number of her works, Weldon's narrative deliberately communicates an ambiguous reading of the power-source. Essentially a postmodernist (although rarely regarded as such except by a few feminist critics), Fay Weldon's feminist stance takes its effectiveness from her ability to 'defamiliarize' the customary material of her novels—which tends at one level to be concerned with women who are socially and culturally victims. Her work constantly displays an admiration for the strength of human will—which, Weldon suggests, when combined with a certain amount of confidence and luck can be powerfully transforming.

Weldon's novel *The Heart of the Country* ends with the narrator/character setting fire to a float during the local carnival procession. Sonia, too, is a relative of Ruth the She-Devil, though her machinations are altogether more subtle than Ruth's. The float represents the West Avon Estate Agents, Dealers and Auctioneers, and becomes a symbol of power relations within the novel, as it is prepared by the women who are paid 'pin-money' by the two men who dominate, sexually and economically, the text and the town.

> The float was ninety feet long. At one end, fifteen feet high and hewn out of balsa wood ... was the image of a kindly estate agent. He held a giant key in an outstretched hand, which would slowly rise and fall as the float moved. Over the other end loomed a noble auctioneer, whose hammer would similarly rise and fall, as its owner turned his smiling head from side to side. Standing firm enough along the edges of the float were ranged the frontages of ideal homes, but not yet completed with the expected lace curtains and pot plants. Standing behind each house was to be an ideal housewife (circa 1955) in frilly apron waving a feather duster ... with a happy smile (*Heart of the Country*, p. 181).

In the event, the women, inspired by the narrator/character Sonia, have other ideas. At the head of the float, the women place the recognizable, scowling figure of the auctioneer, Angus, indeed raising and lowering his hammer, while at the other end is a larger than life-size version of Arthur—who is constructed waving a recognizable key to the back room of his shop where he 'entertains' his female visitors. The float makes significant impact on the small town, especially when the women arrange to have the music changed from "White Christmas" to Pete Seeger singing "Little Boxes"! And the climax of the novel occurs when Sonia, narrator/protagonist, Ruth's counterpart, sets fire to the auctioneer's effigy and delivers an oration in the midst of the conflagration on the evils of male power.

> I told them about the wickedness of men, and the wretchedness of women. I told them they were being had, cheated, conned. That they were the poor and the helpless, and the robber barons were all around...That they lived here in the heart of the country in the shadow of cruise missiles, in the breeze of Hickly Point. That it was up to the women to fight back, because the men had lost their nerve...
> (p. 184).

Unfortunately for Sonia, although the rest of the women jump from the float unharmed, the woman who is dressed as Mrs Housewife Princess does not jump, but is burned to death, and Sonia ends up in a mental institution, in line with all those nineteenth-century heroines of romantic fiction whose acts of rebellion were similarly rewarded.

Here in this text Weldon is using as a sign a festival such as Carnival with all its attached traditions and connotations to challenge and re-write cultural expectations.

The concept of carnivalism is an essential element of Russian Formalist Mikhail Bakhtin's theory of literature, for, of all forms, he considers the novel to be saturated with the carnival spirit. He suggests (*The Problem of Dostoevsky's Poetics*) that Carnival offers "a flexible form of vision" with the carnival spirit proclaiming "the jolly relativity of everything", offering:

> ...the chance to have a new outlook on the world, to realise the relative nature of all that exists, and to enter a completely new order of things (p. 80).

In effect, what carnival does is to suspend customary hierarchical structures and conventional behavior so that things normally separate and distinct are brought together. The larger-than-life elevated figures on the carnival float display at one level the hierarchical status of the two men, while simultaneously offering satiric opportunities in the moving parts—the key and the hammer signifying the phallic and economic 'tools' of the trade of male power. This element of the ridiculous was clearly not lost on the waiting crowd! Also characteristic of the carnivalistic perspectives is the focus placed on abnormal states of mind, which include various mental illnesses, breakdowns and dreams and nightmares. These occurrences might, as Bahktin suggests, give people an insight into "the dialogical attitude of man to himself", that is they "contribute to the destruction of his integrity and finalizedness" by revealing the possibility of becoming "a different person". (Bahktin 1968: 34). It is significant that Weldon should end this book with a ritualistic celebration which offers conditions for radical change—yet in line with all of her novels this revolutionary potential is prescribed by the power relations inherent in the status quo. Sonia is simply deemed to be a woman with severe depression who suffers a moment of manic activity, for which she must be punished and rehabilitated through legal and medical sanctions.

The structural anthropologist Levi-Strauss, speaking of the ways in which human beings organize and make sense of their cultural and social worlds, suggests that we categorize things according to their opposites (Levi-Strauss 1969). Thus things only exist—or at least carry meanings in relation to their binary opposites. John Fiske cites as illustration the story of creation (Fiske 1990:117) in which he suggests that Genesis can be read "as the story ... of the creation of cultural categories by which to make sense [of the creation]" so:

> the dark was divided from the light, the earth from the air...and water divided into waters of the sea (infertile) and of the firmament or rain (fertile).

Fiske further suggests that these binary oppositions may be used to explain more abstract and more culturally specific concepts (as in fertile/infertile) while at the same time grounding those explanations in the natural rather than the cultural. Levi-Strauss refers to this as the "logic of the concrete [which is the] fundamental, universal, sense-making process," deriving from "digital codes" within the brain which are "built upon a system of opposed categories" (p. 117).

Though recognizing the difference helps us to make sense of the universe, nature does not in reality divide into neat categories—day fades into night, night into day as a continuing process.

> There is no clear line between the land and the water—the beach, quicksands, mud are all categories that resist neat binary oppositions. (Levi-Strauss 1969:117)

These categories which take their characteristics from both of the binarily opposed ones, Levi-Strauss calls *anomalous categories*—that is, they blur the distinctions between categories making boundaries unclear. Fiske goes on to suggest, that since these categories derive their characteristics from both of the binarily opposed ones, they possess too much meaning—they are "conceptually too powerful". Because they are, in a sense, 'overloaded' with meaning and because they challenge the clear-cut definitions of binary opposites which make 'sense' of our culture, they have to be controlled or 'managed'—typically by being designated the 'sacred' or the 'taboo'. (This concept directly relates to the second definition of tradition taken from the OED—a long-established custom, having almost the force of law). Anomalous categories derive from two sources—nature and culture, with nature always trying to resist the categorization that culture wishes to impose upon it. Fiske suggests that, for example, homosexuality threatens the clarity of gender categories, and since contemporary society demands clear gender identity, it is surrounded with all sorts of legal and moral taboos. The other sort of anomalous category is that constructed by the culture to mediate between two categories when the division between them is difficult to bridge. Thus Christ is both God and Man; sphinxes and werewolves are both man and beast; vampires hover between the living and the dead. The position of storyteller operates within another such mediating anomalous category—and when fictionally created as character/narrator, negotiates a contract with the reader in which her omniscient power can be located within either nature (spirituality/magical) or culture (materiality/ physicality). The narrator/character in *Growing Rich* reflects on her authorial 'power':

> Sometimes I wonder whether it is I myself, sitting in my window who control their [heroines'] lives, and not just fate; I, who set Driver (the devil) and Bernard Bellamy down the tree-lined road to encounter the girls as they walked home from the little station of Fenedge Halt. Perhaps it was I myself who, on a bored day, initiated the trouble between Kim and Audrey, the melding of Count Capinski in Mavis's mind, to Alan's distress, and rendered Andy unemployed and Raelene miserable and did it irresponsibly, and all just to liven things up a little down here on Landsfield Crescent: a Bad Fairy, after all, not in the least Good.
> But then I remember that a sense of omnipotence can be a symptom of mental illness, and put the notion out of my mind. I live in fear of going mad, just to add to my other troubles (p. 8).

Weldon frequently draws attention to the fictive position of the author—consciously persuading the reader to enter into the traditional relationship with a wise and sympathetic storyteller, while at the same time offering a special contract to the reader in the reader-writer relationship. For example, she is sometimes a disabled narrator; in *The President's Child* she is blind—the blind 'seer' or wise Sphinx whose vision is almost limitless through powerful increases in sensory perception. Here again she links the modern-day world to that of magic and myth. In *Growing Rich* the storyteller is wheelchair-bound—an incapacity which affords her opportunity to develop "the art of seeing through walls, overhearing what could not be heard." She has "nothing else to do but develop these arts" (p. 7). It is not insignificant that, in dealing with a cultural perception of the 'disabled' Weldon foregrounds, with her mythical allusions, the concept of 'different *ability*'. With disarming self-deprecation and disingenuousness the narrator adds, tellingly, "When you think you can see through your neighbors' walls what is fact and what is fiction is hard to distinguish." The art of fiction-writing is just that—an art, and there are nearly always two stories to be gleaned from Weldon's texts—the tale of those observed by the narrator and the story of the artist/teller herself. The reader is offered the dual expectation, that not only will something happen of interest to the characters that the teller has drawn to our attention but that, echoing Scheherezade, something equally momentous and interesting will also happen to the teller once she has completed her narrative task. In the case of *The President's Child* sight is restored once the story has been told—similarly the paralysis which has confined the narrator of *Growing Rich* to a wheelchair 'miraculously' disappears at the end of the novel when her role as Good/Bad Fairy ceases its relevance to the lives of the three chief protagonists.

Similarly, the teller herself is acknowledged as a transforming agent, a spinner of tales which may have a basis in reality but which are changed through her art into fiction—the *fabula*, the elemental objective essentials of the story-line become changed in the narrative process into the *sujet*, or *diegesis* becomes *discours*. I mention this antithetical list not so much to bludgeon with terminology, but to illustrate the ways in which formalist and structuralist poetics establish patterns of oppositional pairings within which the writer must negotiate a position from which to communicate to the reader.

This self-conscious recognition of a transforming craft is openly acknowledged by Weldon as she continuously navigates between the real and the fabulous in her novels. It is both theme and process. *The Heart of the Country*, written in 1987, might suggest from its title a tale of a rural idyll, a sweet old-fashioned pastoral scene. The town, called Eddon Gurney, is not so far removed from the Garden of Eden after all. Yet he novel—which relates a series of sexual encounters and infidelities reminiscent of a game of musical chairs—begins firmly in the pragmatic land of domestic realism with a marriage in difficulties:

> Oh, the wages of sin!
>   Natalie Harris sinned, and her husband Harry left for work one fine morning and didn't come back (p. 1).

Nonetheless, here, as is frequently the case elsewhere in her work, the location carries the suggestion of primeval influences brought into sharp conflict with the modern world:

Mind you, I'm not suprised the Harris household was in trouble. It lived in yet another shadow, being equidistant from the Mendip Mast and Glastonbury Tor. This latter is the solid, ancient hummocky hill which dominates the flat lands in the Somerset Southwest, and from some angles looks like a lady's breast. It's tipped by a crumbling tower, which those who are determined claim looks like that breast's erect nipple. So you could say if you are determined—and many who live around here are—that the Mast was male and the Tor was female: certainly the Mast is modern and the Tor is ancient. The Tor transmits as well, if you ask me, though rather fitfully: probably alpha waves from King Arthur's sleeping brain. The great king is buried in the grounds of Glastonbury Abbey, at the foot of the Tor; not dead, they say, but sleeping, to wake in the hour of England's need. And this is it, if you ask me. So the alpha waves have been hotting up lately, and he's stirring alright, and what with the Tor transmitting its mystic messages of oneness, allness, wholeness, and so forth, and the mast streaming out Dallas and Robin Day, it's not suprising the Harris household quivered and shook and broke into little bits. Well, that's the only excuse I can think of for Harry Harris, who wasn't a bad guy, really. Just panicky about his life and his business, which was failing (p. 3).

This novel presents us with a narrator/character who is as much the 'outsider' as her disabled counterparts in the other works. Sonia (she of the arsonist tendencies) is an abandoned wife, an impoverished woman struggling to bring up her children on welfare—but there is also the strong suggestion that she has lesbian inclinations, and within a novel which foregrounds as theme and context a merry-go-round of heterosexual activity, her sexuality sets Sonia apart. She becomes the narrator, speaking for victim women—but she can only do this in the guise of madness as she reflects, retrospectively, on the carnival parade.

Sonia wanted justice. Sonia wanted to get to the root of things. Sonia bore a grudge. Sonia knew the history of the carnival—all those afternoons with Edwina, hanging about, out of the cold in the Folk Museum, had not been wasted. Sonia wanted her past to catch up with her present. Sonia hated men. Sonia hated men in the same ways that Angus and Arthur, Harry, Stephen and Alec, to name but a few, hated women. It's just that men have power and women don't, so men smile and kiss women and hardly know they hate them, even when they hurt them, and women like Sonia, who hop around the world with as many limbs tied as children, turn shrill and desperate and go mad so the men can see them coming and get out in time. Maenads, harridans, hags, witches—don't look at the Medusa sir, or you'll see yourself in her mirror eyes and turn to stone! Harpy hair and writhing snakes! Shall I tear out a snatch of my hair and hand it to you? Would you like that? No?

A pill please. I must finish the (not, note, MY) story (p. 185).

The ultimate irony here, as elsewhere in her novels, is that the ending promises to be happy, even for Sonia. The other women move around the available men, and settle into various relationships with equanimity. Sonia's therapist falls in love with her and offers her marriage—which she rejects, for her "Happy endings are not so easy." She "must go on changing the world, rescuing the country. There is no time left for frivolity" (p. 199).

Nonetheless, most of Weldon's novels end with a validation of the romance narrative, the fairy-tale transformation. Women still strive to be beautiful and though men may be brutes, as in *The Beauty and the Beast*, 'love' (accompanied by a good helping of lust) is the transforming agency which turns brutality and bestiality into the beauty of true romance. So concludes the romance narrative—which, given the power relations between men and women, and the market pressures of romance ideology, frequently proves irresistible to women. And the happy endings in Weldon are successfully 'marketed'—packaged, all loose ends tied up and, once that task is complete, the teller is able to become 'whole'—though this wholeness is qualified and prescribed, acknowledging the compromise suggested by the Levi-Strauss categorizations. At the end of *Growing Rich* Weldon as teller/character states that:

> ...I was not sure that I would have time to study the stars and learn their names now that I had to take my place in normal society. My disability allowance had ceased. I would have to find a job, or write a novel: something (p. 249).

Economic pressures and the need to survive means that she must forego her amateur tale-spinning status in order to join the 'professional' storytellers in the modern consumer world of the free market!

Women writers such as Weldon have done much to reclaim the power of magic and its association with women. She re-writes the old myths which affirmed cultural and social positions of subservience within a patriarchal order, celebrating transgression, subverting, and offering alternative visions which assert the position of women as powerful, able themselves to transform. This is nowhere more evident than in her own position as the teller of tales, where she inherits a cultural tradition which *does* place women at its center. In a high-pressure consumer market her books are almost always in the best-seller lists in Britain, and she retails very well abroad. Many of her narratives have been adapted for television and film. Weldon very successfully 'markets' tradition, while at the same time demanding of her many readers that they too should acknowledge myth and magic as a process in which Bahktin's 'possibilities of difference' might offer a new sense of self. Her women characters cannot magically change the social and cultural structures of the world in which they live, but they are frequently shown to have powers which can radically modify their own lives. Weldon's novels demonstrate the fact that alternative 'readings' of the modern material world are vital in maintaining a precarious equilibrium of understanding. Ursula Le Guin in her book *The Language of the Night* (1979) argues the vital importance of this reinvestment:

> Those who refuse to listen to dragons are probably doomed to spend their lives acting out the nightmares of politicians.

REFERENCES

Bahktin, M. 1968. *Rabelais and His World*. Translated by Helene Iswolski. Cambridge: Harvard University Press.

Fiske, J. 1990. *Introduction to Communication Studies*. London: Routledge.

Le Guin, U. 1979. *The Language of the Night: Essays on Fantasy and Science Fiction*, edited by Susan Wood. London: Petigree.

Levi-Strauss, C. 1969. *The Raw and the Cooked*. New York: Harper.

Weldon, F. 1984.*Life and Loves of a She-Devil*. London: Coronet.

———.1992.*The Heart of the Country*. London: Vintage. (First published by Hutchinson, 1987).

———.1992.*Growing Rich*. London: Flamingo.

Wisker, G. 1994. *It's My Party*. London: Pluto Press.

Folklore in Use 2, 115–129 (1994)

The Selling of Arthur: Popular Culture and the Arthurian Legend[1]

Juliette Wood

The origins of the Arthurian industry are as difficult to pin down as the King himself. The *Historia Brittonum*, a ninth-century treatise written by Nennius, is the earliest known collection of supposedly historical information on King Arthur. It includes what may be described as the earliest Arthurian tourist brochure in the list of *Mirabilia* (wonders) appended to the end. The locations of these *Mirabilia*, coincidently, are mostly still identifiable in what are today the counties of Mid, South and West Glamorgan and what was then the Welsh Border.[2]

The twelfth-century historian Giraldus Cambrensis may have observed an industrial flowering when he described the exhumation of graves attributed to Arthur and Guenevere at Glastonbury Abbey in 1191 (Brengle 1964:5–11). However, I will concentrate in this article on more recent Arthuriana, using as the starting point a drawing of a cross, now lost, which was allegedly discovered under Arthur's coffin during that exhumation. The drawing, by the antiquarian William Camden, was made in 1607. It depicts what was thought to be an actual relic, something vested with importance because of a literal or physical association with the already legendary leader, and perhaps the drawing marks a transition in the Arthurian industry, because subsequent relics have an association increasingly more symbolic than real with a figure rapidly becoming more mythic than historic.

[1]This paper was originally given as an illustrated talk accompanied by over seventy images associated with Arthurian popular culture. This is intended as part of a book-length study and the present article gives an overview of some of the areas of past and contemporary Arthurian interest in the field of popular culture. References to Arthurian chronicles and romances are not in this instance given to edited texts in the original language, but to more readily available versions.

[2][*Editor's note*: the region in which the conference at which this paper was given was held.]

This paper is not concerned with the historicity of Arthur, or the historical accuracy of the goods, images and stories about him that have developed since Camden's time. The cross depicted by Camden may in fact have been a forgery perpetrated by the monks at Glastonbury to exploit the pilgrimage market. It may have been encouraged by Norman kings who hoped to dispel a Welsh millennial belief in the possibility of Arthur's return. It may even be a Tudor forgery.

The discovery of Arthur's grave was a potent subject. It was imaginatively recreated in a drawing by the Scots artist John Hamilton Mortimer in about 1767. About that time, the 'ancient British landscape' began to interest antiquarian scholars. Mortimer's figures are dressed in classical costumes which locate Arthur, even at this early date, in the context of Druid-as-philosopher, more recent examples of which are discussed elsewhere in this volume by Leslie Jones (pp. 000–000) and Marion Bowman (pp. 000–000). Merlin is depicted as a wiseman and megaliths are seen as druidic temples. It was only ten years later that Thomas Warton called the 'Roundtable' displayed at Winchester a 'druidic frame'. The Winchester table was probably less druidic frame than a Plantagenet creation inspired by Arthurian enthusiasm. It was later repainted by Henry VIII to impress a visiting French monarch. The image of Arthur on the table itself is a representation of the Tudor king *par excellence*.[3] Henry VIII and his daughter Elizabeth I both enjoyed a certain amount of Arthurian role-playing, and both used Arthur as part of the mythic construct of a Britain which was becoming more important politically and economically. While some Tudor historians were trying to find geographical and historical proof for his existence, Arthur was entering the realm of symbolic discourse.

This discourse was part of the market of ideas and images associated with a powerful elite, but the themes of chivalry and knightly honor introduced by the popularity of medieval romances presaged the creation of a series of fellowships imitative of the knights of the Roundtable which created alternative elites: knightly orders such as the Garter, the French order of the Star, and contemporary charity fellowships such as the fraternal organization in Britain known as the Round Table, which actually uses an image of the Winchester table as a logo. (Girouard 1981)

---

[3]The Winchester Roundtable is first mentioned by the antiquarian Hardynge in the late fifteenth century. Its origins are unknown though often speculated on. The official pamphlet is restrained in its claims, but writers such as Loomis (1991) and Weston have speculated about possible Celtic origins or occult uses, and the souvenir shop at Winchester in 1991 was full of neo-Celtic jewelry and a wide selection of New Age publications.

For those wanting material, portable and collectable Roundtable imagery for domestic use, there is a New Age Arthurian Tarot card deck on the market which shows the Roundtable suspended over Stonehenge (Matthews 1990). There is also china—a series of decorative plates produced by Minton reproduces the words written around the edge of the Winchester table as a border for each plate. An Arthurian figure covered in Celtic interlace designs occupies the center.

Finally, in a note on Roundtable-linked behavior, a former student sent me a newspaper cutting accompanied by a note telling me that "flexi-history is alive and well". The cutting describes how an environmental protestor was apprehended after a "spring solstice" celebration in front of the Roundtable.

Since this can only be a brief survey, I would like to move rapidly from a consideration of the uses of the Roundtable to a quick sketch of the development of some icons which originate from the different versions of the Arthurian story. I will quickly explore swords, shields, grails and dragons, wizards and women (whether fair or foul). This survey begins with literary and pictorial images before concluding with a look at what is literally on the market—or possibly in the toy stores today.

EXCALIBUR AND THE SWORD IN THE STONE

The image of Excalibur was used by Carling Black Label in a recent advertising campaign on British television. The Arthurian advertisement was based visually on the ending of John Boorman's film *Excalibur*, and hinges on the emergence of a synchronized swim team in place of the Lady of the Lake. A visual joke occurs when one of the knights, distracted by the glamorous swimmers, leans on the sword which slides back into the stone. Here the observer needs to know the specifics of the story. However, according to medieval chronicles and romances, Excalibur is given to Arthur by the Lady of the Lake *after* the sword from the stone is broken (Hopkins 1993:19–20). The first mention of the sword as test for the future leader occurs in Robert de Boron's romance. The text indicates that the sword is embedded in an anvil not a stone. In a medieval illustration the sword is positioned as if it had cleft the anvil. Attempts have been made to link Arthur's sword with the Samartians, or the Cathars or the Templars. In this context and in many visual depictions, Excalibur is seen as buried vertically. The illustration of Robert de Boron's romance is one strand of visual tradition which portrays it differently.

Even the cover illustrations of the many more recent books about

Arthur and Arthurian themes are an interesting study. The iconography adapts to changing markets. In the cover illustration for Rosemary Sutcliff's *Sword at Sunset* the sword is a recognizably medieval weapon, while in a 1935 rewrite of Arthurian tales (Winder 1935) the influence of the Welsh story of the fairy bride from Llyn y fan fach can be seen in an illustration of the figure walking on the water and in the caption, and Glastonbury Tor can be seen in the background. The heroic act gives way to magic.

A ceramic figure of Arthur pulling a sword from the stone is very Celtic in inspiration and the advertising copy calls the sword Excalibur. Lest we assume this is a wholly modern misunderstanding, there is a Middle English poem *Arthour and Merlin* which also calls the sword in the stone Excalibur. Evidently alternative views of aspects of Arthur's legend, assuming that De Boron's text can be used as a touchstone, were an early development. Wilkinson's offers a more historical approach to Arthur's sword, "an exact replica" of the Roman *spatha*, the appropriate weapon for the fifth-century warlord. A romantic image of the sword entwined with vines and a reference to Arthur sleeping in a cave in Wales appear in a local guidebook (anon. 1987). While a fifteenth-century woodcut collapses the final episodes of Morte D'Arthur into one frame. The king's knights mourn on the shore; Arthur sits in the boat bound for Avalon, the arm catches the sword; but a bit of charming realism has crept in. A duck startled by the arm reaching out of the water, paddles furiously away.

THE SHIELD OF ARTHUR

Arthur's shield also develops both in the chronicles and romances and in the popular imagination. In *Historia Brittonum*, the substantial earliest Arthurian source and in Geoffrey of Monmouth's *Historia Regum Brittaniae* and much of the chronicle tradition, the image of the Virgin is depicted on Arthur's shield, as in the splendid picture of the king in the Langtoft Chronicle, but the continental tradition assigns Arthur and his knights heraldic devices as if they were real knights and they can be recognized in illustrations by these devices. Arthur here usually has a shield with three crowns.

These heraldic devices were reasonably constant in both verbal description and illustration as long as the chivalric context remained viable. Another Arthurian heraldic reference occurs in the coats of arms created for the Tudor monarchs with quartering showing their descent from Arthur. Modern illustration is more fanciful in depicting the devices on shields, it becomes part of the decoration rather than a device for recognition. However the most recent Arthurian revival is closely linked with popular ideas about the Celts and Arthur's shield is usually covered with Celtic interlace designs, as for example on the plate and ceramic figure of Arthur produced recently by Minton.

Arthur's regalia as a whole, is interesting in terms of subsequent developments in popular culture. Geoffrey of Monmouth gives a list of some eight named objects which belong to Arthur, he is followed in this by both Wace and Layamon (Brengle 1964:12); the objects include sword, shield, knife, mantle, ship etc. The names derive ultimately from Welsh via Geoffrey's curious Latin equivalents, and there is a substantial tradition in Welsh of a list of Arthur's regalia.

THE HOLY GRAIL

Traditions about the Grail are a study in themselves, and these brief observations only hint at a vast popular appeal. There are several objects which claim to be the actual Grail and become the focus for popular religious activity and local interest. One such is the so-called Antioch Chalice now in the Metropolitan Museum of Art in New York, another is the Nanteos Cup held for many years at the Nanteos estate outside Aberystwyth and a third is in Valencia, Spain. The Grail has been all things to all men, everything from the chalice and knife used in the Byzantine mass rite, a Celtic cup of rebirth, a symbol of hidden pagan rituals, the tomb in which Christ's body was placed or, to the survivors of the Merovingian dynasty, a symbol of the offspring of Christ and Mary Magdalen surviving from Merovingian France to the present day.

THE STORY OF TWO DRAGONS

Lego toys link a dragon, a charmingly domesticated one named Ogwen who defends Castle Carreg, with Merlin in their Castle Series and, in that same series, the Black Knight sails under a Red Dragon banner. The story of the two dragons, one red and one white, first appears in *Historia Brittonum*, connected with Ambrosius Aurelianus. Geoffrey's text introduces Merlin and the dragons become part of Arthurian literature. An illustration from a Lambeth Palace manuscript shows two beautifully detailed dragons about to fight. The scene includes a pool and several onlookers and closely follows the text. In popular works of history and folklore, much is made of Henry VII marching under a Red Dragon pennant; the Red Dragon did not really become common as part of the Welsh flag or its popular history until the nineteenth century. As part of the revival and recreation of an appropriate Welsh past it stands on the dome of Cardiff's City Hall and is a popular image on Welsh tourist gifts from cuddly toys to pottery and, in a manifestation unique to Welsh-speaking culture, the *tafod*, the dragon's tongue, is the symbol of the Cymdeithas yr laith (Welsh language society). A series of collectors' dolls dresses the Arthur figure in carefully researched fifth-century style clothing. His crown is based on Byzantine mosaic portraits like those at Ravenna, but the design on his cloak is a dramatic Red Dragon. The image of the dragon underlines the fact that popular Arthuriana is a somewhat arbitrary category. Arthurian imagery often exists in the context of wider concerns—magic and mysticism in the late twentieth century, the medieval revival of the nineteenth and the political and intellectual climate of the Tudor period.

MERLIN

In medieval texts Merlin is master of a vast but unspecific power. He is sometimes called a sage or a magus, but is visually very different from the modern conception of the magus. The Egerton Chronicle depicts him at the building of Stonehenge. He is bearded but a vigorous and young-looking figure than a magus should be. A broadly similar depiction occurs in connection with the *Histoire de Merlin*. In a woodcut illustrating Heywood's Elizabethan play, however, he is a kind of Friar Tuck, beardless and rotund. This woodcut includes the two dragons in the background as well.

But the image of Merlin as a wise, bearded magus is probably the result of a Victorian revival of interest in Arthurian matters (Hughes 1989:1–35). Tennyson certainly contributed to this view of Merlin, and Gustave Dore's illustrations and Burne-Jones' paintings realize the image of a Romantic, melancholy sage. Visually the bearded sage owes much to antiquarian interest in the druids as philosophical figures. Tennyson's Merlin is still a rational magician, one who thinks before he shape-shifts. While Tennyson's *The Idylls of the King* is hardly popular culture, it was influential and embodied widely held Victorian attitudes to the Middle Ages. The thinking magician is found in twentieth-century fiction. Hal Foster's Prince Valiant remembers Merlin's words before going into a mysterious cave "A mystery when solved is mere facts / Magic, when explained is but science" (Foster 1989:9). Edgar Rice Burroughs and Andre Norton's heroes get sent to Mars and the Witchworld respectively by a dignified figure who shows them the Siege Perilous, (Norton 1963) a facilitator like the one in tales of Arthur as a sleeping hero, not the powerful magus of modern sword and sorcery epics.

Modern popular images of Merlin (and he has never been so popular) carry on the visual tradition started in Victorian times, but present an altogether more magical figure. Wizards can be purchased in every size and at every price. Tall gaunt figures with stern looks, clad in flowing robes carrying books of magic, staves, wands, crystals and swords are available in any size and material. Often they are accompanied by an owl, a detail supplied by T.H. White's popular fantasy. Walt Disney's Merlin, from his animation of T.H. White's *Sword in the Stone*, is a cuddly magician rather like Cinderella's fairy godmother with a beard. Disney is such an important influence on popular perceptions of fairy tales that it is worth pointing out that benevolent Otherworld figures are often cute and cuddly—for example the fairy godmothers in both *Cinderella* and *Sleeping Beauty*. The negative Otherworld figures are often long and gaunt and medieval looking, as for example, the Wicked Fairy in *Sleeping Beauty* with her stylized horned headdress, and the wizard in *The Sorcerer's Apprentice*, who is not unlike some of these wizard figures so popular now.

ARTHURIAN WOMEN

The changing character of the female figures in Arthurian commercial tradition needs to be seen in the context of new interest in feminine spirituality. (Fries 1990:207–222) As such it is really outside the scope of this article except to say that, as with so many popular developments, the shift begins much earlier than it seems. Modern Arthurian fiction has often exploited the potential of Arthurian women (Fries 1990:207–222). However, in the longest running Arthurian comic strip, *Prince Valiant*, the women are strongly defined. Prince Valiant's wife and twin daughters are, when the occasion demands, spitfires who frequently best the male characters. This, however, seemed too much for the Hollywood film version of *Prince Valiant* in the 1950s in which the heroine is rather vapid (Harty 1991). There does seem to be an ambiguity toward the female figures. William Russell Flint's illustrations depict women figures as central subjects (for example the schoolgirl Morgan practicing her magic on one of the good sisters) but many Arthurian retellings depict the women as beautifully dressed with downcast eyes. The strength of the Arthurian female is something which is recognized, if only sporadically. Revlon advertised skincare products in the 1960s using the image of a woman's face swathed in glittering fabric resembling chain mail, while in the 1990s a vitamin company linked healthy strength with a woman in body-molded armor.

ARTHURIAN TOYS

Since the nineteenth century the Arthurian legend has become part of children's literature. (Curry 1990: 149-164) The manageress of a large children's bookshop was confident that Arthurian children's books always sold well and managers in several toy shops described Arthurian toys as "steady sellers".

Arthurian toys are essentially a product of Victorian attitudes to childhood and the subsequent merchandizing of those attitudes. An Arthurian toy theater was available from the *Boys Magazine*, a pulp publication produced by the Victorians for "the lower orders", full of bad jokes, puzzles and derring-do. It contains a serialized comical history of England, based distantly on Geoffrey of Monmouth. The tone is illustrated by this summary of Mordred's character, "a more dreadful man you cannot imagine". The same issue has a cartoon of Arthur killing the Giant on Mont St Michel. The illustrations for the Toy Theater show the influence of the aesthetic movement, and the text is wonderfully melodramatic with stirring lines like "Unhand her, How dare you treat a British lady so". The tone is anti-German, with the 'real' Britons opposing the invaders. Merlin is bearded, but not particularly magus-like. Arthur sports the three Prince of Wales ostrich feathers. A modern version without the ideological overtones and without specific Arthurian characters nevertheless contains the same elements of a good knights, bad knights, ladies and excruciating prose. "Hawks talons!" exclaims the villain.

Arthurian dolls are comparatively rare. Specialist doll makers and hand-made dolls for school projects are made as Arthurian characters. The American firm, Effanbee, produced a Guenivere doll as part of an historical series in the 1970s and the Peggy Nesbitt Company produced an Arthurian knights and ladies series about the same time. King Arthur and Sir Lancelot Action-Man dolls were modeled on the film actors Richard Harris and Franco Nero and sold in the 1960s.

Toy soldiers are a natural development for popular Arthuriana, but soldiers representing specific Arthurian characters are surprisingly hard to find. Any knightly figure can be adapted to the legend. Toy shop assistants frequently reported that Britains' Toy Soldiers were bought for children because of an interest in Arthur. Timko produced a special set in the 1940s called 'The Knights of the Round Table' which contains Lancelot, Mordred and Agravaine with details such as real feathers. One of the 'Knights in Armor' introduced by Britains in the 1930s and produced until the mid-sixties, although not named, may be Arthurian.

The figure is a splendidly detailed mounted knight with an elaborate golden dragon on his helmet. Geoffrey of Monmouth says Uther Pendragon's helmet was surmounted by a golden dragon. Model enthusiasts are usually history buffs, and this is such an elaborate feature, that it is not too outlandish to suggest the designer knew of Geoffrey's description in some form. The toy soldiers produced by Britains and similar firms are usually based on historical sources. The 1993 catalogue lists Champion, Shield and Storm knights whose overall appearance has changed little since they were introduced. However in the 1980s even Britains seems to have caught the fantasy bug, at least to the point of introducing a dragon on wheels.

Model makers favor historical wars with those of the last century the most popular. The *Men at Arms* Series has a volume entitled *Arthur and the Anglo-Saxon Wars* (Nicolle and McBride 1984) which establishes a fifth-century historical setting made popular by archeology and history. Everything is based on some archeological find, museum pieces or carving, well documented with speculation kept to a minimum. A sixth-century cavalryman is described "As far as we can judge this Celtic warrior was the reality behind the 'Arthurian knight'." The description of the Welsh tribal warrior begins "Even less is known about the tribal warriors of the Celtic highlands". The prose here is a great deal more cautious than some academic writing about the Celts (Nicolle and McBride 1984:35).

Fantasy is a major theme in popular culture of the late twentieth century. Arthurian fiction and fantasy fiction in general is a major component in the development of role-playing games. Arthurian games are small group within an enormous field. *Prince Valiant* exists in role-playing form but *Pendragon* is the most popular with a large and devoted following. A recent survey of fantasy games distinguishes the Arthurian ones from more fantastical games such as *Dungeons and Dragons* by emphasizing that the code of chivalry is more important in the former. One of the creators of Pendragon says "the game system is revolutionary because it addresses issues heretofore ignored in role-playing, including family life; morality and behavior ... time passage, changing customs and ideals" (Schick 1991:78) The creators of these games are aware of sources, but deliberately break the rules and combine old, modern, historical and fictional sources to create ever more complex and challenging games.

Although it makes no direct use of Arthurian characters, The Model Workshop combines the medieval and the fantastic in a game that can either be role-directed or improvised by the players. The Brettonians, the main human characters, with their evocative name, are very like Malory's knights and conform visually to what used to be known as 'The High Middle Ages'.

Arthurian themes, knights, heroic deeds, even the feudal worlds of the Middle Ages, have contributed enormously to comic book images and ideas (Slocum and Stewart 1990:291–308). The most notable Arthurian comic is Hal Foster's forty-five-year-old epic *Prince Valiant*. Foster was a graphic artist trained in Chicago in the 1930s and influenced by Twain, Lanier, and the heroic literature available in the United States at that time. He used a graphic novel style not a strip cartoon. The drawing and writing were taken over first by John Cullen Murphy in the 1970s and more recently by Murphy's son. It has its own cult following, the Friends of Prince Valiant. The story has been made into a film and is currently a children's Saturday morning cartoon. It has attracted the interest of several Arthurian scholars. Hal Foster's striking artwork is totally anachronistic and mixes periods with abandon, but it has a kind of integrity in that the figures are consistent within themselves. The costumes do not defy gravity as so much modern fantasy art does, and the figures do not have distorted muscles like so many comics. Because of this, the anachronisms do not jar. The storylines echo the visuals. Although loaded with stereotypes—the drunken, brawling Viking, the sleazy Saracen, the noble savage, the untrustworthy oriental—individual characters are able to overcome their stereotype. Lacking are Twain's negative attitudes to the medieval, Lanier's ethical ideals and the somewhat racist heroicism of many of the fantasy novels popular at the time. What one gets are medieval versions of Damon Runyon and O. Henry stories. Interesting too is the comparative lack of magic, certainly by the standards of modern fantasy writing. This is not say that the story and images do not change. Recently one of Valiant's daughters married an Italian, a nice balance to the earlier prevalence of Northern European types. The medieval landscape has changed. In an adventure of the late 1940s, Val comes upon a castle which looks like Neuschwanstein. In 1993 the fortifications resemble Harlech in Wales, although according to the text this castle was built by the Romans on the Saxon shore. In the same episode Valiant builds a fort which looks like a cross between Cadbury and Danebury Rings.

The *Illustrated Classic* comic book series did a King Arthur story and the graphic novel style, itself a cult fantasy art, does occasionally turn up in children's books. One has a rather rare image of Arthur asleep in his cave (Wilkes 1989). *Camelot 3000*, an adult comic, does wonderfully camp things with the story. The author's knowledge of Arthur goes back, he says, to a college course in Arthurian literature and his treatment is very much *Rex futurus* (Barr and Bolland 1988). Arthur and his men are called back from their sleep to be the messianic hope. Tristan comes back as a woman and falls in love with Isolde anyway. The final pages visually summarize the sources of the imagery. They are Marvel comic heroes with large doses of Tolkien, Lovecraft and the Celtic revival. Arthur is a blond, Saxon-looking king, Merlin the noble magus/wizard, Tristan and Isolde a lesbian couple. In Morgan the influence of Tolkien's Shelob is strong, Excalibur is the sword taken and returned to the stone and the little monster who brandishes it is very like Lovecraft's Chthulu.

In the United States the Kennedy years have become known as the Camelot Era and, with Jackie Kennedy's recent death, the phrase has re-appeared. *Vanity Fair* described her on its cover as "Camelot's Queen". On her marriage to Onassis, *Life* ran an article entitled "Goodbye Camelot, Hello Scorpios." That mine of popular American culture, *The National Enquirer* (a weekly tabloid newspaper), reports that just after the assassination Jackie herself told the journalist Theodore White that *Camelot* was the President's favorite musical, in particular the final verse of the theme song "Don't let it be forgot...". Kennedy's presidency seemed aimed at a long stay in the White House and one suspects a certain narrative re-arrangement in declaring his fondness for a verse so poignantly appropriate for a man soon to be assassinated. Popular journalism added a 'sleeping hero' in the form of Kennedy on a Greek island kept at the expense of Onassis, and the story has been collected from American University students. It makes wonderful newspaper copy and book titles. At least twenty titles, mostly collections of Kennedy photos, appeared between the years 1972–1980.

Interesting links with popular Arthuriana exist in an area even more ephemeral than politics, namely fashion. The influence is not a direct one however. Soft cut high-waisted clothes were popular before either the "Camelot" musical or the film. Guenevere's costume worn in the 1964 New York production of the musical looks more like a fashionable wedding dress of the day than historical costume. One of the Fifth Avenue shops in New York once used a medieval theme in its windows. One of the figures was a 'knight in armor', but the female figure in the same window wore, not a costume, but a high fashion dress in medieval style. Medieval-inspired wedding clothes were popular throughout the mid-sixties to mid-seventies. Both Princess Anne and her attendant wore dresses adapted from historical costume. A revival of the musical *Camelot* in the 1970s sparked an article on 'Camelot Look' hairstyles in a woman's magazine. Medieval influences in women's dress are not new. The author's personal collection includes a 1950s beaded version of the round 'Juliet' cap and printed velvet fabrics designed in the 1930s by Maria Gallega, an associate of Fortuny. However the 1960s saw both a revival of these trends and their mass marketing by firms such as Laura Ashley in Britain and Jessica McClintock in America.

Arthurian collectibles are popular once more, especially in connection with New Age marketing and many have a decidedly Celtic slant.

Postcards, figures, t-shirt logos, jewelry and posters all use Arthurian motifs. Some historicism still remains, such as a ceramic head of Sir Lancelot (Bossons Co.) in 'historically' correct sixth-century Roman armor, as he would have looked "defending Christianity against the heathen Saxons in the Celtic areas of the British Isles". It seems churlish to point out that the first mention of Lancelot is in a twelfth-century romance by Chretien de Troyes. The bulk of contemporary Arthuriana is New Age Celtic in its inspiration. An Arthurian Tarot appeared recently combining Arthurian characters, Celtic designs, Goddess imagery and New Age commentary (Matthews 1989). Several Arthurian-inspired packs have been produced, all within the last 50 years. A link between the Tarot and Arthur, via the Grail Quest, was proposed by A.E. Waite, a member of the Order of the Golden Dawn, about 1910 in three books: *The Hidden Church of the Holy Grail*; *The Holy Grail*, *The Galahad Quest in Medieval Literature* and, to a lesser extent, *The Pictorial Key to the Tarot* (the pack produced by Pamela Colman Smith in collaboration with Waite is vaguely medieval but not Arthurian). Jessie Weston uses the Arthur/tarot/Grail link in *From Ritual to Romance* and T.S. Eliot gets it from her. (Grayson 1992:1–80). Indeed the links between turn-of-the-century occult theory and the Celtic revival provide as important background to modern New Age thinking about Arthurian and Celtic literature and this has ramifications for Arthuriana.

The more expensive modern Arthuriana bears comparison with some medieval objects with Arthurian themes. Exquisitely crafted objects such as mirrors and boxes usually made of ivory were adorned with Arthurian themes. Lovers, such as Tristan and Isolde, were popular and appropriate for items such as mirror backs and jewel containers. This kind of object is usually treated in the context of fine arts. Some scholars see a direct relation between these objects and the texts; others suggest that they could be interpretations of artistic motifs by master craftsmen, and not indicate much of significance about the extent to which tales were known. What they do indicate is that production for a specialized Arthurian market is not entirely new.

ARTHURIAN ADVERTISING

I would like to end by discussing Arthurian names in advertising. They can convey any mixture of nobility, dignity, mystery and romance. In 1925 the South Western Railway added Arthurian nameplates to its N15-class locomotives. In total fifty engines received Arthurian names. One was allotted the name *Sir Mordred*, but this was later changed. Plant varieties are occasionally given Arthurian names. Kelways Nurseries offered a yellow iris called *Sangraal* and a peony called *King Arthur* in their 1994 catalogue. Ships, at least in the British navy, have been given Arthurian names. An eighteenth-century figurehead depicts Sir Lancelot, his helmet adorned with Prince of Wales ostrich feathers. An oil platform called Avalon is in the Dutch sector of the North Sea oil field, one of many Arthurian names to mark Mobil Oil platforms. The streets on the Thornhill Estate, a housing development in Cardiff, are called by Arthurian names. Cardiff businesses include Merlin computers, bakery, engineering, film processing, fireplace, hotel, motors, recycling, tool and die companies. An Arthurian name provides added recognition where several businesses of the same type operate in a reasonably small area. Occasionally they are poetically appropriate, as in *Excalibur Hand Tools* of Cardiff.

As an advertising logo, Arthurian names combine instant recognizability with a whole range of positive qualities which, like the traditions, are infinitely adaptable. The wizard, as used in computer advertising, transforms the technicalities of the computer into magic. *Merlyn liqueur* exploits not just the link between wizards and drink, but of Welsh products as well. Merlin was baptized in Brecon water and pure Welsh cream (two ingredients) and Excalibur was fixed in a boulder from the Brecon Beacons, the location of the distillery. In February 1994 McDonald's UK urged us to "Join in the Quest/Seek out a Lucky Golden Straw", while in May *Chic* magazine assured us that "Finding the perfect mascara can seem like a quest for the Holy Grail". Kerbigrips in *Punch* in the 1950s combined Lancelot and Guenevere with Rapunzel and hairpins. Political and advertising cartoons exploit readers knowledge of the legend to comment on a implied situation. For example a furniture company advertised 'Ye Sale' with Arthur and his knights in a showroom of odd-shaped tables claiming "We had our hearts set on something round".

Like the *Once and Future King*, examples of Arthurian goods seem eternal. Popular culture is a good index of general cultural attitudes. And with something as popular and adaptable as Arthur the possibilities are limitless.

REFERENCES

Barr, Mike W. and Brian Bolland. 1988. *Camelot 3000*. New York: DC Comics.

Brengle, Richard, ed. 1964. *Arthur, King of Britain*. New York: Appleton, Century, Crofts.

Bromwich, Rachel. 1978. *Trioedd Ynys Prydein*. Cardiff: The Welsh Triads

University of Wales Press.

Clynes, Michael. 1993. *The Grail Murders, Being the Third Journal of Sir Roger Shallot concerning certain wicked conspiracies and horrible murders perpetrated in the reign of Henry VIII*. London: Headline.

Cooper, Richard. 1987. *Knights of God*. London: Lion.

Curry, Jane L. 1990. Children's Reading and the Arthurian Tales. In *King Arthur Through the Ages, Vol. 11*, ed. V. Lagorio and M.L. Day, pp. 149–164. New York: Garland.

Dumville, David N. 1977. Sub-Roman Britain: History and Legend. *History* 62:173–192.

Foster, Harold R. 1989 [1941-42]. *Prince Valiant*. Vol. 6. Westlake Village, CA: Fantagraphic Books.

———. 1990 [1943-44]. *Prince Valiant*. Vol. 8. Westlake Village, CA: Fantagraphic Books.

Fries, Maureen. 1990. Trends in the Modern Arthurian Novel. In *King Arthur Through the Ages, Vol. 11*, ed. V. Lagorio and M.L. Day, pp. 207-222. New York: Garland.

Gooodrich, Peter H. 1989. Modern Merlinus: An Aerial Survey (Bibliographic Essay). In *The Figure of Merlin in the Nineteenth and Twentieth Centuries*, ed. J. Watson and M. Freis, pp. 175–197. Lampeter: Edwin Mellon.

Girouard, Mark. 1981. *The Return to Camelot: Chivalry and the English Gentleman*. New Haven: Yale University Press.

Grayson, Janet. 1992. In Quest of Jessie Weston. *Arthurian Literature* xi:1–80.

Harty, Kevin. 1991. *Cinema Arthuriana: Essays on Arthurian Film*. Garland New York.

Haycock, Marged. 1983–1984. Preiddeu Annwn and the figure of Taiesin. *Studia Celtica* 18–19:52–78.

Hopkins, Andrea. 1993. *Chronicles of King Arthur*. London: Collins and Brown.

Hughes, Linda K. 1989. Ilusion and Reality: Merlin as Image of the Artist in Tennyson, Dore, Burne-Jones and Beardsley. In *The Figure of Merlin in the Nineteenth and Twentieth Centuries*, ed. J. Watson and M. Freis, pp. 1–35. Lampeter: Edwin Mellon.

Knight, Stephen. 1983. *Arthurian Literature and Society*. Basingstoke: Macmillan Press.

Kyle, Duncan. 1978. *Black Camelot*. London: William Collins.

Loomis, R.S. 1991 [1963]. *The Grail: From Celtic Myth to Christian Symbol*. Princeton: Princeton Unviersity Press.

Matthews, Caitlin and John Matthews. 1990. *The Arthurian Tarot*. Illustrated by Miranda Gray. Wellingborough: The Aquarian Press.

Matthew, John. 1990. *Household of the Grail.* Wellingborough: The Aquarian Press.

Norton, Andre. 1963. *Witch World.* New York: Ace Books.

Nicolle, David and McBride, Angus. 1984. *Arthur and the Anglo-Saxon Wars.* Men at Arms Series. London: Osprey.

Treharne, R.F. 1967. *The Glastonbury Legends: Joseph of Arimethea, the Holy Grail and King Arthur.* London: The Cresset Press.

Schick, Lawrence. 1991. *Heroic Worlds: A History and Guide to Role-Playing Games.* Buffalo, New York: Prometheus Books.

Simpson, Roger. 1990. Camelot Regained. *Arthurian Studies* 21:55–113.

Slocum, Sally K. and Alan Stewart. 1990. Heroes in Four Colours: The Arthurian Legend in Comic Strips and Books. In *King Arthur Through the Ages, Vol. 11,* ed. V. Lagorio and M.L. Day, pp. 291-308. New York: Garland.

Waite, A.E. 1961 [1911]. *The Holy Grail. The Galahad Question in Arthurian Literature.* New York: University Books.

Weston, Jessie. 1992. *From Ritual to Romance.* Princeton: Princeton Unviersity Press.

Westwood, Jennifer. 1992. *Gothick Cornwall.* Devon: Shire Publications.

Wilkes, Angela, ed. 1989. *The Adventures of King Arthur.* Illustrated by Peter Dennis. London: Usborne Publishing.

Winder, Blanche. 1935. *King Arthur and his Knights.* Illustrated by H.G. Thecher. London and Melbourne: Ward Lock & Co Ltd.

Folklore in Use 2, 131–142 (1994)

The Emergence of the Druid as Celtic Shaman

Leslie Jones

Druidism must surely hold the crown for being, not only the most invented tradition in the Western world, but the most re-invented. In the public arena, skeptics point out that eye-witness accounts of the religion of the pre-Christian Celts would probably fill less than ten pages of text; those who claim to be modern druids usually counter to the effect that druidism has been retained in disguise as an aspect of "Celtic" Christianity or as the shattered jewel of myth and folklore. The Roman historian Tacitus portrayed the druids as doomed rebels against the Empire, the Irish hagiographer Muirchú as second-rate magicians whose pyrotechnics were no match for the true faith. Yet even in these earliest references to druidism, no druid speaks to us directly. It is a mediated discourse, suspect from its inception given that our sources are not only *not* druids, but are the enemies of druids. This tabula semi-rasa has, however, provided a wall on which the graffiti artists of history and religion have felt invited, indeed compelled to scrawl.

The latest incarnation of the druid, one which has arisen only in the last five years or so, is the druid as Celtic shaman. The inspiration for this incarnation seems to have arisen from a combination of Michael Harner's *The Way of the Shaman* (1980) and Nikolai Tolstoy's *The Quest for Merlin* (1985). Both of these authors have drawn heavily on serious academic research in order to write books for an educated yet non-expert audience; the same population that produces many followers of New Age belief systems.

While there is much to criticize in Tolstoy, he must be credited with putting together a reasonable and popular demonstration of an idea that has been floating around in academic Celtic Studies for quite some time: the realization that there is a shamanistic element in Celtic mythology which persisted at least into the medieval era (see Caerwyn Williams 1971; Nagy 1981). This train of inquiry has also been interestingly developed by Carlo Ginzberg in *Ecstacies* (1991) and by Tom Cowan in *Fire in the Head* (1993). Neither of these books, however, claims to teach the reader how to *be* a Celtic shaman.

Harner's work, meanwhile, has become the cornerstone of New Age shamanistic practice. The rhetorical strategy of combining anthropological data, myth, personal experience narrative, and visualization exercises, the emphasis on drumming as a tool for accessing alternative states of consciousness, and a listing of workshops and mail-order sources for further information, has become the paradigm for most current mystical handbooks, whether they attempt to teach druidism or Native American shamanism.

A typical example of these books is John Matthews' *The Celtic Shaman: A Handbook* (1992), a book that might just has easily have been titled *How to Become a Druid in the Comfort and Privacy of Your Own Living Room.* Following Harner's narrative structure, Matthews relates how, in his quest for spiritual fulfillment, he came to the United States and encountered a Native American shaman who gave him a vision and told him to go back and discover his own native *British* shamanic tradition.[1] Matthews then explains the Celtic shamanistic cosmology, calendar, geography, and deities, interspersed with meditations and visualizations meant to help the reader find a power animal and a spirit guide (terms taken directly from Native American shamanism), to reconnect with the natural world, to practice divination, and to acquire the accoutrements of shamanism: a medicine bag in Native American terms, a crane bag—drawing on Fenian tradition—in Matthews' system; an Indian drum for Harner, a bodhran for Matthews. To give him credit, he does state that Celtic shamanism is *not* druidism (a disclaimer I suspect is lost on many readers), but his concentration on Taliesin as the archetypal *shaman*/poet confuses the issue, since in earlier formulations of druidism Taliesin is usually presented as the archetypal *druid*/poet.[2]

Not only does Matthews syncretize Celtic material to North American shamanism, he also syncretizes to the Germanic worldview found in the

---

[1]This encounter is interesting. Native Americans have become increasingly vocal in their displeasure with shaman-wanna-bes usurping their indigenous faith. Matthews presents the Native American shaman as a wise and encouraging soul who inspires Matthews to seek his own native roots, but in the political context one cannot help but wonder if he was really telling Matthews to just back off and leave him alone.

[2]Patrick Ford discusses the history of the image of Taliesin in the introduction to his edition of *Ystoria Taliesin* (1992:1–64). The more widely-known and, alas, influential take on the subject, however, is Robert Graves' notorious *The White Goddess* (1948). As an inspiration for poetry, *The White Goddess* has more than proved its worth, but as a guide to Celtic mythology, it is a complete fantasy.

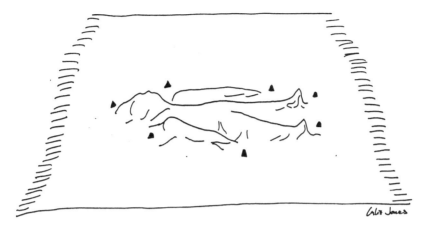

Figure 1. "The Visionary Journey." The shamanic initiate meditates under a rug or blanket, surrounded by seven stones of power. (After Matthews 1991:102, Fig. 14.)

Eddas. This is characteristic of the monism of most New Age thought, which sees all religions as different versions of the same basic faith. His figure of the Celtic shamanistic cosmos (Matthews 1991:36, Fig. 2) looks exactly like the image of the Eddic Yggdrasil, with nice little pan-Celtic touches such as the figure of Cernunnos replacing the Norns at the base of the World Tree, ringing "Middle-Earth" with a henge, and the whole cosmos enclosed in the shell of a hazelnut of wisdom taken again from Fenian tradition. He comments of this cosmology, "It is not unlike many other such maps from different cultures, but it bears an unmistakable aura of 'Celticity'!" (Matthews 1992:35). Given that such a cosmology exists nowhere in extant Celtic lore, given that Matthews has essentially made it all up, albeit by a process of bricolage rather than out of whole cloth, such coincidence seems less than remarkable.

Visualization exercises are the key element in all do-it-yourself shamanism manuals. One cannot help but wonder exactly where Matthews' meditations are leading the seeker, however. Granted the druids were noted as tree-worshippers, but one of these exercises literally calls for you to go out and hug a tree. Hug several trees. Become friends with trees. *Be* a tree. And presumably, do all of this with a straight face. The loopiest exercise, however, is the visionary journey to the Other-world (Fig. 1). While obviously influenced by Martin Martin's famous description of early eighteenth-century Scottish poets composing poetry with a plaid wrapped around their head and a stone on their belly (cited in Caerwyn Williams 1971:36), this picture pushes the whole notion of do-it-yourself shamanism to absurdity. Evidently, not only can you become a Celtic shaman in the comfort and privacy of your own home, but you can do it by merely crawling under the carpet. Doesn't it make you sneeze? Or is one of the perks of shamanism that you get a more powerful vacuum cleaner than I have? Perhaps New Age shamanism should forget power animals and concentrate on power tools.

The rhetorical style of the visualizations in these manuals also raises some purely technical reservations about their effectiveness. Harner's exercises are generally very short on the page, and give only broad outlines as instructions: basically he says, Go to a place you think of as an entrance to the underworld and go down; see what you find there (Harner 1990:31-32) The details of the visualization come from the initiate's own subconscious. Matthews' visualizations not only detail what the place will look like, but he tells you what you will feel, how you will react to what you find there, even what "spontaneous" thoughts will occur to you on the journey. For instance, in the exercise of "The Blindfold Hunter":

> Then, in the distance, you seem to see something. At first you think it is an illusion, because there is no light to reveal anything ... But the feeling grows stronger, and with it comes a new certainty. There, in the distance, is light! Only a dim greyness which would not, in normal circumstances, pass for light at all, but it is enough to show you that you are sitting on a grassy knoll in the middle of an unknown landscape...
>
> You strain your sense to "see" where the light is coming from. There, below the mound, you gradually make out the shape of a well-head. The light is coming from the well ... So desperate are you by now that you scramble down to the lip of the well and look in...
>
> At one there comes such a blast of light that you reel back from the well, blinded by the violence of the illumination. It is at that moment, confused and befuddled, caught between the two extremes of uttermost darkness and brilliant light, that you hear the answer to your question, as loudly as though it had been shouted up to you from within the well ... Desperately you scrabble at the blindfold which you are suddenly aware is around your eyes ... (Matthews 1991:158).

Wisdom from a well and *imbas forosna* ('great light that illuminates') are pervasive themes in Celtic mythology and may have some shamanic basis. But they can be manifested in many forms. Why is *this* form used by Matthews? And if it works for him as a shaman, who is he to say that it will work for everyone? Furthermore, given that this is a self-study course, how are you supposed to accomplish these complex journeys? You cannot read a book while in a shamanic state of consciousness, and if you read the exercise into a tape recorder, how do you know how long the journey will take? Will your spirit guide hit "Pause" at the appropriate moment?

These inner quests of the Celtic shaman are fuzzy and warm, exciting but not particularly dangerous, like the pony ride at the amusement park; the magical Otherworld quivers with anticipation when it realizes that you want to come out and play; Balor of the Evil Eye and the Fomoire are nowhere to be found, or if they do rear their ugly heads you will overcome them with ease because, as Cybill Shepard reminds devotees of L'Oreal hair dye, "you're worth it". Shamans have more fun. The encounter with the Otherworld basically comes down to sightseeing and acquiring souvenirs, albeit on a spiritual plane. Even Matthews' visualization of death and rebirth makes no mention of pain or anxiety. Harner's Jívaro shamanism is more than a little scary—if you screw up you could lose your soul. In Matthews' Celtic shamanism, you have little to lose besides your dignity.

A less explicitly shamanic and more straightforwardly druidic work is *The Elements of the Druid Tradition* (1991) by Philip Carr-Gomm, himself the Chosen Chief of the Order of Bards, Ovates, and Druids (OBOD) and therefore, one would assume, someone who knows what he is talking about. Carr-Gomm's agenda is to explain the basic outlines of druidism to those interested in the topic but uninitiated into its mysteries. Interestingly, while this particular druidic order claims to have roots going back to Atlantis, and while the modern organization dates back to those crackpots of the Enlightenment responsible for the neo-druidic craze of the eighteenth century, Carr-Gomm's narrative follows the shamanic paradigm we find in both Harner and Matthews: the personal experience narrative of an encounter with a wise teacher, the initiation process, the outline of the basic mystical principles, and the visualization exercises, with an appendix listing sources for further enlightenment, in this case featuring the postal study course offered by OBOD itself.

Indeed, the pervasiveness of the Harner shamanic paradigm becomes clear when we look at Ross Nichols' *Book of Druidry* (1990). This book, published posthumously, is in the main a collection of unconnected writings by the previous Chosen Chief of the OBOD, with an introduction by Carr-Gomm. By telling the story of his own relationship with Nichols, Carr-Gomm provides the personal experience and initiation narratives, while Nichols' writings, actually reflecting a more old-fashioned, hierarchical vision of druidism, provide the esoteric wisdom element, and the scripts for rituals take the place of visualization exercises.

For both Matthews and Carr-Gomm the best reason to become a druid in this day and age is because the old Celtic religion was in tune with the natural world, and we need to reconnect with nature and care for the earth in this techno-bound, post-modern, pre-apocalyptic age of ours. The Indian shamanism propounded by Harner focusses on healing the individual; this Celtic shamanism claims to aim for healing the earth.

There is a subtext to this heal-the-earth-through-druidry program, however, that is somewhat disturbing. In the 1980s, Ronald Reagan's first Secretary of the Interior, James Watts, was viewed with considerable alarm by some environmentalists because he was a fundamentalist Christian, and this was believed to produce a mindset that regarded the earth as something put here by God with which mankind might do anything he damn well pleased, and in fact that it was our Christian duty to get as much out of the earth as we could without any thought of the long-term consequences. The fact that Watts' policies confirmed this view is beside the point at the moment; the point is that people who believe themselves to be diametrically opposed to officials such as Watts and to the Judeo-Christian Master-of-the-Universe model of man's place on the planet assume that their spiritual opposition to the worst of culture makes them automatically One With Nature. That is the explicit message of the druid-as-shaman. But implicit in these handbooks of druidry is the same old assumption of man's dominance over nature—just now we will be good Massas rather than bad. The Celtic shaman turns out to be an eco-nanny, running around cleaning up the messes with which the more childish amongst us have polluted our once-Edenic nursery. Matthews even ends most visualizations by reminding you to say "thank you" to everyone you met on your journey; no doubt he would advise including a hanky in your crane bag.

But what is it that druidism, or any other esoteric system, really offers? It offers power, knowledge as power. This is the one constant in druidic reinvention. What changes is the way in which that power is envisaged. William Stukeley, one of the great druidic inventors of all time, envisaged a druidism that was nothing more than Anglicanism waiting to happen (Piggott 1989:123–146). Eighteenth-century writers invented a druidic hierarchy through which one progressed much as one worked one's way up from the vicarage to the Bishop's Palace (Piggott 1975:123–182; Hutton 1991:139–200). This was a druidism that regarded power as residing in social interaction, in "interest," as they called it then, in networking, as we call it now.

This social druidism provided the operative paradigm until really quite recently. Looking at, for instance, Tadhg MacCrossan's *Sacred Cauldron* (1991), we find a druidism that is geared towards providing an alternative family for the practitioner. The focus is on rituals that bring people together for a common activity, just as the Church has traditionally provided an arena for social activity within the community in addition to its religious mission. MacCrossan even suggests that the festivals of Samhain, Imbolc, Beltaine and Lughnasa be celebrated at the nearest weekend so as to avoid conflict with clan members' work schedules.

Shamanism offers power but it is a lonely power. Shamans, real shamans, are not the life and soul of the party; indeed, they are often alienated from their own society, forever straddling two worlds and wholly belonging to neither. The shaman has been called the "wounded healer" because so often the shamanic call comes in the form of an illness, whether mental or physical, that cannot be treated any other way than by undergoing shamanic initiation. To look at this phenomenon positively, it means that the shaman has personal experience of the ailments of his patients, much as a psychiatrist must undergo analysis as part of his own training. However, let us consider the warning that prefaces *The Celtic Shaman*:

> This book constitutes an exploration of ancient shamanic techniques normally undertaken with a qualified teacher. The reader is therefore solely responsible for his or her own action in undertaking the training offered herein. It should also be clearly understood that the methods and techniques described in this book are not a substitute for either psychological or medical treatment (Matthews 1991:n.p.)

A similar disclaimer prefaces Harner's work. While this may merely reflect the self-protective instincts of the publisher's lawyers, it also suggests that the publishers, indeed the authors expect that their readers are people who glorify their social alienation as a symptom of "special-ness" and who may, in fact, be attracted to the idea of supernatural power as a compensation for powerlessness in other realms.

Shamanic druidism offers a religious paradigm that at least theoretical-ly does not have any institutional structure, reflecting a general distrust of bureaucracy that pervades many levels of society today. The idea that you can learn to be a shaman from books, inner spirit guides and other ethereal teachers seems analogous to the "enthusiastic" religions that swept through Britain in the eighteenth and early nineteenth centuries, oddly enough coinciding with the last great druidic revival (Jenkins 1987:342–426, 1988:42–75; Morgan 1981, 1983). However, the druidism emerging from that revival emphasized the druid as a scientist-astrono-mer who already held keys to a natural world that Enlightenment science was only just beginning to rediscover; it was the ultimate organized, and organizing, religion. Shamanic druids are as inspired as were early Quakers and Baptists, and depend on their own inner sense of conviction to lead them rather than the teachings of an established church.

Whereas many Enlightenment neo-druids seem to have been attracted to it by a combination of a feeling of the emptiness of establishment religion and a revulsion against the emotional excesses of enthusiasm, what seems to attract people to druidism today is a sense of the emptiness of science itself. A recent survey in the United States found that, whereas it has often been assumed that New Age pagans are most likely to be Roman Catholics looking for a new form of ritual, in fact, in proportion to their representation in the population at large, Jews are twice as likely to become neo-pagans as Christians, and people with no formal religious background are also a large contingent (Kelly 1992:145–146). The New Age seems to be supplying, not replacing, religion for those who feel themselves out of the mainstream.

But to return to the theme of power, shamanism is a double-edged sword. On the one hand, it seems to be lacking power if power is defined as a bad thing, an aspect of oppression and restriction and institutionalization. But it also presents itself as something that must be more powerful than science, because science cannot explain it, and science is the most powerful force we know today, especially if we do not have a strong sense of God to begin with, especially if science is, as so many have suggested, our religion. The New Age may be the Enthusiasm of the late twentieth-century in more ways than one. Shamanic druids can have their cake and eat it too; all the perks of power without any of the tedious paperwork.

Both ethnographic data on shamanism and early Celtic literature present the reader with material that is very alien to the mainstream Western European world-view, although parts of it may surface in marginalized forms. The Otherworld is not a postmortem heaven or hell, it is right behind your shoulder and may jump you at any moment. People become animals, animals talk, severed heads talk, otherworldly speech is hard to understand but it means more that way. Supernatural beings eviscerate you, wash your guts, and stuff your head with crystals, and this doesn't kill you, it just turns your head into a cosmic radio. Black pterodactyls try to con you into believing that they are the masters of the universe; the god who offers to help you in battle has actually set up the war so he can sleep with your wife. Shamanic initiation is supposed literally to blow your mind; it breaks your brain and puts the pieces back together so you see the world in a different way; and if Nikolai Tolstoy did nothing else he corralled all the mad Celtic poets into the same tree for a moment so that we can see just how many of them there really are.

But all of this incomprehensible, dreamlike, frightening and beautiful and dangerous and tantalizing *stuff* has been homogenized and sweetened by these manuals of Celtic shamanism. I would not go so far as to call them Disneyfied, but they Tolkienize Celtic myth into something readily assimilated by an audience accustomed to late twentieth-century fantasy and science fiction. Matthews' Arianrhod is "a woman of such beauty and delicacy that she seems almost transparent ... her face is as perfect as a crystal rose." She says to the seeker, "you are come to seek that which is to be" (Matthews 1991:28). This is a far cry from the sharp-tongued Arianrhod, the mother from hell, whom we find in the Fourth Branch of the Mabinogi. For all their claims of gender equality, these handbooks turn the prickly, witty, independent Celtic goddesses into Victorian Angels in the House. For all their reference to Jungian archetypes, they ignore Jung's acknowledgement that in order to find wisdom and healing within ourselves, we have to come to terms with the evil and danger that lies there as well. For all its multicultural monism, the very idea of a Celtic shaman renews that old identification of the Celts and Indians, whether they all be envisioned as Lost Tribes of Israel or aboriginal wisemen of the woods. This is an identification that, historically, has not done much to illuminate the culture of either the Celts or the Indians, and I am not sure it is really worthwhile reviving it now.

Under the guise of offering/providing an alternative to already compromised institutional power structures, these druidic handbooks actually reaffirm mainstream stereotypes of race and gender. But perhaps most unforgivably, they emasculate the poet-shaman at the very source of his power, in the realm of language. Compare the words of a New Age Celtic shaman with those of an ancient Irish poet. The first is a prayer to earth suggested by Matthews.

> May the earth receive my words
> May the earth receive them
> May the earth listen to them
> May the earth believe them
> May the earth respond to them
>
> I ask the earth to hear
> I ask the earth to listen
> I ask the earth to respond
> I ask the earth to bear witness
> I ask the earth to bear witness
>
> That her children have not forgotten
> That her children have not forgotten
> That her children still respond
> That her children still can hear
> That her children will not forget
> That her children are sorry
>
> And I ask the earth to bear witness
> That we shall make amends
> That we shall restore her
> That we shall continue to love her
> That we shall continue to love her
> That we shall remake what we have unmade
> That we shall put back what we have taken

That we shall listen to her voice

May the earth receive my words
May the earth receive them
May the earth listen to them
May the earth believe them
May the earth respond to them (Matthews 1991:139).

This is a humble, indeed passive-aggressive little piece in pseudo-tribal diction; it may be a shamanic chant, or it may be a monologue by Richard Lewis. Its repetitive form may invoke an altered state of consciousness, but that state will probably be sleep. The shaman takes on the voice of an apologetic child who has thoughtlessly smashed an heirloom after being told for the hundredth time not to run through the dining room. In this context, promises never to do it again seem to carry little weight.

In contrast, Amergin's invocation of Ireland, from the *Lebor Gabala Erenn*, retains its power even in translation.

I invoke the land of Ireland.
Much-coursed be the fertile sea,
Fertile be the fruit-strewn mountain,
Fruit-strewn be the showery wood,
Showery be the river of waterfalls,
Of waterfalls be the lake of deep pools,
Deep-pooled be the hilltop well,
A well of tribes be the assembly,
An assembly of the kings be Tara,
Tara be the hill of tribes,
The tribes of the Sons of Mil,
Of Mil be the ships, the barks,
Let the lofty bark be Ireland,
Lofty Ireland, darkly sung,
An incantation of great cunning;
The great cunning of the wives of Bres,
The wives of Bres of Buaigne;
The great lady of Ireland,
Eremon has conquered her,
Ir and Eber have invoked her,
I invoke the land of Ireland
(trans. R.A.S. Macalister and John MacNeill, in Cross and Slover 1969:19).

The interwoven structure of the lines embodies the interconnectedness of nature and culture from which the poet draws his own power. The fertile sea, the well of tribes, the incantation, the wives of Bres, Eriu herself, Amergin himself, all are tied together with words and through these words reality itself is altered—or at least, it is in the story. J.E. Caerwyn

Williams called the druidic bards of medieval Ireland "Lords of the Word in a world in which words had not yet lost their magic power" (1971:10). If there is anything shamanic in Celtic religion, it is not "greenness" but this power over and power through language. If people really want to become Celtic shamans in this day and age, perhaps they should crawl out from under the carpet and sign up for a poetry workshop.

REFERENCES

Caerwyn Williams, J.E. 1971. *The Court Poet in Medieval Ireland*. Sir John Rhys Memorial Lecture. *Proceedings of the British Academy*, vol. 57. London: Oxford University Press.

Carr-Gomm, Philip. 1991. *The Elements of the Druid Tradition*. Shaftesbury: Element Books.

Cowan, Tom. 1993. *Fire in the Head: Shamanism and the Celtic Spirit*. New York: Harper.

Cross, Tom Peate and Charles Slover, eds. 1969. *Ancient Irish Tales*. Totowa, NJ: Barnes and Noble.

Ford, Patrick, ed. 1992. *Ystoria Taliesin*. Cardiff: University of Wales Press.

Ginzberg, Carlo. 1991. *Ecstacies: Deciphering the Witches' Sabbath*. Raymond Rosenthal, trans. New York: Pantheon. [Work originally published in Italian as *Storia Notturna*, 1989.]

Graves, Robert. 1948. *The White Goddess: A Historical Grammar of Poetic Myth*, amended and enlarged ed. New York: Farrar, Straus, and Giroux.

Harner, Michael. 1990. *The Way of the Shaman*, updated ed. New York: HarperSanFrancisco. [Work originally published 1980.]

Hutton, Ronald. 1991. *The Pagan Religions of the Ancient British Isles: Their Nature and Legacy*. Oxford: Basil Blackwell.

Jenkins, Geraint H. 1987. *The Foundations of Modern Wales: 1642–1780*. Oxford: Oxford University Press.

———. 1988. The New Enthusiasts. In *The Remaking of Wales in the Eighteenth Century*, ed. Trevor Herbert and Gareth Elwyn Jones, pp. 43-75. Cardiff: University of Wales Press.

Kelly, Aidan A. 1992. Update on Neopagan Witchcraft in America. In *Perspectives on the New Age*, ed. James R. Lewis and J. Gordon Melton, pp. 136-151. Albany: SUNY Press.

MacCrossan, Tadhg. 1991. *The Sacred Cauldron: Secrets of the Druids*. St Paul: Llewellyn.

Matthews, John. 1991. *The Celtic Shaman: A Handbook*. Shaftesbury: Element Books.

Morgan, Prys. 1981. *The Eighteenth-Century Renaissance*. Llandybie: Christopher Davies.

———. 1983. From a Death to a View: The Hunt for the Welsh Past in the Romantic Period. In *The Invention of Tradition*, ed. Eric Hobsbawm and Terence Ranger, pp. 43–100. Cambridge: Cambridge University Press.

Nagy, Joseph Falaky. 1981. Shamanic Aspects of the *Bruidhean* Tale. *History of Religions* 20:302–22.

Nichols, Ross. 1990. *The Book of Druidry: History, Sites, Wisdom*. London: Aquarian Press.

Piggott, Stuart. 1975. *The Druids*. New York: Thames and Hudson.

Piggott, Stuart. 1989. *Ancient Britons and the Antiquarian Imagination: Ideas from the Renaissance to the Regency*. New York: Thames and Hudson.

Tolstoy, Nikolai. 1985. *The Quest for Merlin*. Boston: Little, Brown.

Folklore in Use 2, 143–152 (1994)

The Commodification of the Celt: New Age/Neo-Pagan Consumerism

Marion Bowman

There have been periods of fascination with Celts and Druids in the past, whether among seventeenth- and eighteenth-century antiquarians or nineteenth-century Romantics; indeed, perhaps we can say that there has been a history of continuous interest in Celts, simply marked by peaks and troughs. However, I think it is fair to say that there have never been the same spiritual implications for such a large number of people, nor such marketing opportunities, as we are witnessing now.

In order to look at the Commodification of the Celt in the context of New Age and Neo-pagan consumerism, it will be helpful to preface my comments with a thumbnail sketch of contemporary New Age and Neo-pagan thought in Britain, and the image of Celts within it, as well as saying a little about how the Druids fit into this scheme of things. The role of Celts and Druids in some Christian circles will also be briefly discussed. I shall then demonstrate something of the variety of products, producers and sales outlets to which these ideas have given rise.

The present speculations and beliefs concerning Celts and Druids represent an important aspect of contemporary religion, particularly in relation to New Age, Neo-Paganism and Christianity (Bowman 1993). They also raise issues relating to postmodernity, elective affinity, religion and identity, religion and nationality, the return of the noble savage and of course market forces and consumer choice. So, what is happening and why?

Paganism[1] in its many forms is enjoying a great expansion of popularity in Britain at present. Pagans are looking to Britain's pre-Christian past and, depending on your viewpoint, they are recovering, re-discovering or reinventing the religious life of their ancestors. For many the attraction of paganism is as Green Religion/Eco-religion; Christianity and scientific rationalism are seen to have failed in terms of

---

[1]Having established that I am discussing the contemporary phenomenon of Neo-paganism, I will hereinafter use the terms Pagan/Paganism, as that is how contemporary Neo-Pagans refer to themselves.

cherishing and looking after the earth, with disastrous results. Many Pagans are thus seeking to re-establish a symbiotic relationship with Mother Earth, to be in touch with the natural world, indeed respecting and revering the planet instead of exploiting it. One way Pagans express their closeness to the earth and a greater awareness of the seasonal cycle is through the celebration of the eight-fold calendar of equinoxes and solstices, plus *Samhain, Imbolc, Beltane* and *Lughnasadh*. All this creates a need (indeed, a market) for information, for literature, for artifacts, for a past—or a suitable version of the past—that they can reclaim. For many Pagans in Britain, as that past is perceived to be Celtic, the present becomes Celtic too.

Varied as New Age is, one of the few ideas that we can say is common to most New Agers is that of a new age. There is the commonly held view that we are at a critical time in the history of the world, perhaps indeed in the history of the universe. Of paramount importance in New Age thinking is the discovery of the Self; the emphasis is on individuals taking responsibility for their own religious life, undertaking their own spiritual quest. Spirituality is a very personal matter, therefore the individual progresses at his/her own pace and by the means most suited to that individual. There can be no one set path for everyone; you must do what feels right for you. However, individualism is not isolationism. There is a great emphasis on interconnectedness, between all life forms in the universe, between different levels of the spirit world, and between the past and the present.

While in the UK most publicity goes to the counter-cultural wing of New Age in the form of the so-called New Age Travellers, comparatively little attention is paid to the prosperity wing.[2] Many New Agers are affluent and articulate people who assert that it is possible to make a living *and* be spiritual; that there is no point in having high ideals and going bankrupt. This is the age of the soteriological entrepreneur. Each person is an essence of god, but it is legitimate to charge high fees to help people discover that. Spiritual enlightenment can go hand in hand with affluence, as New Age management training and techniques show. In a place like Glastonbury, described as the epicenter of New Age in Britain, a whole New Age spiritual service industry has arisen, including New Age Bed and Breakfast establishments, New Age pilgrimage guides and over a hundred forms of alternative healing. The individual's spiritual quest involves or can involve consumer choice, as the individual decides which workshops, therapies, gurus, literature in which to invest.

---

[2]Paul Heelas has written extensively about the prosperity wing and financial implications of New Age (Heelas 1992, 1993).

In New Age, it has been observed, there are not followers or devotees but clients.

While there are undoubtedly differences between New Age and Paganism, it is fair to say that there is a common theme—humanity has become out of step with the earth personified as Gaia, we are spiritually out of tune with ourselves, with others and with the universe. It is widely held, however, that it was not always so, that in the past our ancestors appreciated the way things were, were in tune with nature, were aware of the sacredness of all existence, knew their place in the great scheme of things. It is for this reason that there is such stress on, and such high status given to, ancient wisdom, esoteric teachings, native wisdom. The Golden Age is located in the untainted, sacralized life of the 'noble savage', and for numerous people in Britain that noble savage is undoubtedly a Celt.

When looking at the Celts, archaeologists, Celticists and historians may be unhappy about gaps in archaeological evidence, unreliability of sources, limits to what they feel can be safely inferred, and the fact that the Celts in the British Isles were not and are not one homogenous group. However, many New Agers and Pagans perceive a self-aware, pan-Celtic culture and worldview, details of which are confidently enumerated. Details of this Celtic past are claimed to be the product of esoterically transmitted wisdom only now coming to light, interpretation of cultural tradition, inspiration and channelling. Channelling—receiving messages from discarnate spirits—and past life regression are particularly significant, as the past comes to the present and vice versa.

The Druids appear in this picture of the Celtic past as a wise priest-hood, ecologically aware custodians of ancient wisdom. Many New Agers and some Pagans believe this ancient wisdom was in fact transmitted to Celtic Christianity in the essentially smooth and harmonious transition from the old religion to the new. The Druids are said to have foreseen the coming of Christianity, even to have welcomed it. The shared knowledge and early co-operation between Druids and Celtic Christians is presented and accepted as fact among many New Agers and contemporary Druids, some Pagans and indeed some Christians. Celtic Christianity is seen as preserving a body of esoteric knowledge, known by the Druids but unknown to other branches of Christianity. Celtic Christianity is generally regarded in New Age and some Druidic circles as having been far more spiritual, more intuitive, more in touch with nature than its Roman counterpart. There can be few other contexts in which the Synod of Whitby (644 AD) is so frequently mentioned and so bitterly regretted. However, it should be recognized that the Celtic church is also being looked to and eulogized by many within mainstream Christianity. The Iona Community has become the inspiration for

Christians within a variety of denominational traditions, and for many
is a sort of icon of Celtic Christianity.

Nor is interest in Celts simply confined to overtly spiritual circles. For
many in Britain the Celts have become Britain's Noble Savages. The
Celts, people on the fringes, instead of being despised, patronized or
pitied for not being in the mainstream, are now seen as less tainted, as
repositories of a spirituality, a sense of tradition, a oneness with nature
that has elsewhere been lost. There is, then, a general interest in and
market for the Celts and things Celtic, although I am concentrating here
on the more specialized spiritual subsection of the clientele.

Within the British Isles, Celtic for many New Age and Pagan adherents
is broadly interpreted to embrace Scots (all Scots), Irish, Welsh, Manx,
Northumbrians, people from the West Country—more or less everyone
who is not, as it were, mainstream southern English. People perceived as
contemporary Celts are to some extent seen as special. In Glastonbury,
a conversation with another Scot was interrupted by a gentleman saying
how thrilled he was to be in the presence of two Celts. Pamela Constantine, founder of the New Romantic Movement, recently wrote to me:

> I think the reason there *is* such a [Celtic] revival is because the human
> spirit has been restricted so long by a society in which science and
> materialism and profit-motive predominate. It has been dammed up
> and is now urgent for expression. It seems to me the Celts have a
> natural ability to reopen the 'magic casements' and to help people
> reconnect with the lost dimensions of themselves.

Meanwhile, those with some sort of Celtic or quasi-Celtic ancestry
frequently use this to help establish their credentials; the co-organizer of
a workshop at a Festival of the Celtic Spirit for example, was described
as 'a Northumbrian Irish Celt exiled in London.' In Bath, Anne Hassett
the clairvoyant has within the past couple of years become Acuthla, the
psychic consultant, 'in honor of her Celtic roots'. Rhiannon Evans, maker
of Designer Celtic Jewelry and t-shirts with the slogan 'Ancient Traditions from the British Celts of Today' drops into her advertising copy:
"All our jewelry is handmade by Welsh-speaking craftsmen at Tregaron
in Wales—one of the last remaining corners of Britain where the Celtic
heritage is still very much of the present time." Basically, if you've got
Celticity, flaunt it.

However, 'Celtic', always an archaeologically, historically, linguistically
tricky label, is presently undergoing re-interpretation at a variety of
levels. What constitutes Celtic is fluid, one might almost say 'up for
grabs'. At the huge Celtic exhibition in Venice in 1991, the Celts were
presented as the first Europeans. Tim Sebastian, Chosen Chief of the
Secular Order of Druids, is of the opinion that ultimately everyone in

Britain is of Celtic descent. For Tim and other Druids, Stonehenge is the great national, British, Celtic monument. Embers Celtic Spirit, who run shops and a mail order catalogue, proclaim "Wherever you are in the British Isles you are surrounded by the Spirit of the Celts, the art, the history and the myths and legends of a civilization whose culture has lasted over 2500 years. The Romans and Vikings came and went, but the Celts remain within the names of towns, villages and areas of Britain. It is our heritage and roots." Besides, the New Age Celt transcends both history and geography: as it was put in a recent New Age magazine, "Being a Celt is like nobility, a thing of spirit not of heritage" (Gannon and Feld 1992). So, as a Glastonbury informant told me "The world is rediscovering Celtic beliefs and being drawn to them".

It is extremely important to realize that while people are ostensibly looking to the past, what happened then is not necessarily what they are concerned with. As one New Age resident of Glastonbury said:

> There's something there, a wonderful ambience, and we can localize it as no one is sure who the Celts really were. It doesn't matter about strict historicity—it sets up a wonderful warm glow of hope, helps you feel more integrated. What we need in the West is a Celtic renaissance.

Some New Agers and Pagans are trying to reconstruct a Celtic past, some are trying to reinterpret a Celtic past to make it relevant to the present, some are creating or reinventing something about which they know little can be proved but which somehow 'feels' right.

There is thus a lot of scope for the construction of a variety of models of what it is to be Celtic and what a Celtic lifestyle might be. There are now many people who might be classified as 'Cardiac Celts': they feel in their heart that they are Celts. Carl Raschke claims that "New Age religion may in many respects be described as the *commodification of the arcane and obscure*" (1992:104) and these cardiac Celts can subscribe to Celtic magazines, acquire Celtic artifacts, go to workshops to learn how to become a Celtic Shaman to confirm their new or newly rediscovered identity.[3] Many Pagans and New Agers are simply 'free range' Celts, who arrive at and express their Celticity in fairly random and individual ways. However, some take being Celtic more seriously than others. Clan Dalriada, for example, is a group of Pagans living on the Isle of Arran, "who have dedicated their lives to living and working the Celtic/Gaelic system of the late Bronze Age (the time we hold to have been the Golden Age of the Celts)." Clan Dalriada also run the Dalriada Celtic Heritage

---

[3]See Leslie Jones, this issue, pp. 000–000.

Society, which aims to promote "a greater awareness of Celtic culture, traditions and beliefs, both of ancient and modern times" in addition to offering a correspondence course on Celtic Paganism. The Order of Bards, Ovates and Druids offers an Open University-style correspondence course in Druidry, while Kaledon Naddair, Director of Studies for the College of Druidism in Edinburgh also runs a training course which he considers sets the standards for 'Genuine Druidism'.

If not wishing to study Celticity formally, the aspiring New Age or Pagan Celt can surround him or herself with Celtic literature, by which I do not necessarily mean curling up with the Mabinogion or some academic, literally uninspired hence uninspiring tome. Writings about the Celts and Celtic spirituality written from specifically New Age/Neo-pagan standpoints abound, and much of such literature should be regarded in the religious studies usage of myth as a 'significant stories', regardless of questions of truth or falsehood. Such books turn up in most New Age and Alternative bookshops, as well as the Mind/Body/Spirit sections of High Street bookshops such as Waterstones. Particularly prolific in this respect are John and Caitlin Matthews, joint presiders of OBOD and authors of numerous books on Arthurian and Celtic topics. Caitlin is described as an "initiator within the Celtic tradition", which captures the apparent need for Celtic roots coupled with the element of personal choice and inspiration which is a hallmark of contemporary religion. Caitlin's *Elements of Celtic Tradition* and *Celtic Book of the Dead*, John's *Celtic Shamanism*, their joint work *The Little Book of Celtic Wisdom* are influential and illustrative of this type of specialist, insider literature. Writings from the late nineteenth-/early twentieth-century Celtic revival are also in vogue in such contexts, and reprints of these appear alongside new editions of *The Mysteries of Britain*, Lewis Spence's "rallying call for a national spiritual regeneration based on the secret rites and traditions of ancient Britain." Meanwhile Clan Dalriada, and small presses up and down the country, produce booklets on such subjects as Celtic Totem Animals, Gods of the Celts and Trees of the Celtic Alphabet. This year will see the publication of Gordon Strachan's much anticipated book, *Jesus the Druid*.

There are numerous magazines serving the New Age and Pagan community, many of which use Celtic themes or artwork or contain specifically Celtic articles from time to time. In addition, there are self-consciously Celtic magazines, such as *Celtic Connections*—"dedicated to all aspects of Celtic culture, especially the arts and crafts", covering Wales, Scotland, Brittany, Ireland, Isle of Man and Catalonia. Clan Dalriada produces *Dalriada Magazine*, which focuses specifically on the Celtic Gaelic tradition, and there are other regional specialist magazines. For those who wish to pursue Celticity more actively, there are workshops and conferences to be attended which explore particular aspects of Celtic tradition and spirituality. There are Festivals of the Celtic Spirit and Celtic Day Schools around the country. In 1991 the Centre for Creation Spirituality at St James's Piccadilly, a noted New Age centre, held a weekend conference entitled 'Exploring Our Celtic Spiritual Roots'. Once a year Caitlin and John Matthews offer a Foundation Course in Celtic Shamanism, limited to only twenty students. This year's course held over two weekends in Bath was an instant sellout, with a waiting list of disappointed would-be shamans hoping for cancellations.

One aspect of the commodification of the Celt is the perceived importance of the craftsperson in the Celtic tradition. Pendragon, a New Age shop in Glastonbury, proclaimed in a press release at the time of its opening:

> [Pendragon] grew out of a deep association with Glastonbury over the years and a desire to see the resurgence of the Celtic spirit, which to us means living in harmony with the Earth, following a path of the spiritual warrior, and bringing again the artist/ craftsperson's importance into the community.

Within Clan Dalriada:

> Every clan member is required to take up a craft of their own choice, be it wood carving, pottery, storytelling or whatever, just as our ancestors within the clan units of old would have done. These traditional crafts are carried out in the spirit of the Old Ways. They are not simply about making a finished product. They are much more than this. Each of the thirty-six crafts is a unique path of self development on the three levels of body, mind and spirit. Each craft is a communion with the Old Ones of these lands. Each craft is like a stepping stone across the waters of the great cosmic sea, as the Celtic spirit moves onwards through many lifetimes in its quest to reach the Summerlands.

Craftwork is thus seen as a Celtic activity, which can increase the spirituality of the maker. However, by extension, the products of such craft can be seen as imbued with Celticity. These objects might have implicit spirituality, but there are also explicit spiritual or inspirational artifacts. Artist and scupltor Simant Bostock, for example, advertises and operates under the rubric 'Spirit of the Ancestors'; in his catalogue he states "My interest in art has always been in it's [sic] magical power as a vehicle of spiritual wisdom, transformation and healing." Bostock produces Celtic Crosses, Celtic Heads, various Celtic Gods, a Celtic Wild Boar and a Celtic Bull. Such items come complete with cards on their history and symbolism.

Contemplating and possessing Celtic art can in itself be elevating;

Courtney Davis has written of *The Little Book of Celtic Designs* by David James: "A little treasure trove of delightful, strong and uplifting images … simply turn the pages … and you will journey through a selection of some truly inspired Celtic pictures." Courtney Davis himself produces the *Celtic Mandalas*, another example of art, inspiration and spirituality combined.

Although it is by no means the first time that religion and the market place have combined, one aspect of New Age and Neo-Paganism is that spirituality meets consumerism. We are in the realm of DIY religion, for which certain shops, mail-order companies, craftspeople, publishers and workshop organizers have become the spiritual equivalents of B&Q, Homebase or Builder's Emporium.

To possess certain items quite literally puts one in touch with the Celts. Many feel the need to acquire or express celticity, and one way this can be achieved is through artifacts. There is no shortage of such purchases and providers, as a browse through the many Celtic craft advertisements in *Celtic Connections,* or a visit to such establishments as Once and Future Celt ("Pagan Paraphernalia, Heathen Hoards, Celtic Crafts, and Goddess Goods") or Wilde Celts ("Pan Celtic Art, inspired by the Golden Age of Celtic Creativity") can confirm. When it comes to commodifying Celticity, there are two main options. One is to make what are perceived as specifically Celtic things—the Celtic Bull, the silver bough—or to offer a specifically Celtic service—training courses in Celtic Paganism, workshops on Celtic Shamanism. The other main option is to take otherwise ordinary or neutral objects and make them Celtic, e.g. Celtic watches, Celtic coasters, Celtic soap, Celtic cards, Celtic notepaper, Celtic t-shirts, Celtic tarot cards, Celtic gloves, Celtic socks, Celtic clocks, Celtic ties. To make something Celtic often simply involves adding some knotwork or some other suitably Celtic-looking motif.

There is undoubtedly a commercial aspect to all this, for Celtic sells, to the general public as well as to specifically New Age and pagan audiences. It is noticeable how much Celtic paraphernalia there is for sale in cathedral and museum giftshops now. The people selling and making such items vary, as do the reasons people have for buying them. I spoke with a Bristol-based woman who sells Celtic jewelry, i.e. brooches, earrings, cufflinks, etc. with Celtic designs on them. Her display at craft fairs includes photocopied explanations of the designs, taken from Courtney Davis's *Art of Celtia.* I had anticipated a personal interest in things Celtic, but the seller revealed that she had been attracted to the material on purely aesthetic grounds—"good design is timeless". She had added the explanatory details in response to customers' questions, as she herself hadn't known, but she felt the explanations seemed to add to the appeal of the jewelry for some people. Something need not be made or sold with a spiritual connection or context or intention, but it can be interpreted as such according to the disposition of the buyer.

Of course, some of what is happening is just clever marketing, a response to a popular trend; but many within the Celtic commodities business are not simply dealing in ethnic chic. Kaledon Naddair's Koelbren Divination Sets and Livewood Koelbren Pens ("Unique Pens, beautiful to handle ... which bear on them the Tree-Wisdom of the Keltic Druids") help to provide a way of making a living with integrity related to his main sphere of interest, the Keltic Druid tradition. Many in the business of selling Celtic artifacts and services do in fact have some sort of mission: Embers Celtic Spirit, in response to my question as to whether they perceived any sort of spiritual aspect to their business or whether it was purely a commercial operation, wrote:

> As regards a 'spiritual' aspect of our business, we are certainly not in it 'just for the money' as the whole area of our business started from a love of the Celts, music, religion (Christianity from the celtic side) etc. There is a growth in Celtic interest and our aim is to further it as it is our roots and heritage in Britain.

The current trend of believing without belonging, the individualizing of religion, again fits well with the spiritual supermarket image of New Age, and by extension some forms of Paganism. Consumerism a matter of individual choice, and in a mobile, fragmented society what were formerly features of a particular group or tribe now have to come in individual portions. Thus workshops enable people to discover their personal totem animal, the individual decides at will to become a Celtic Shaman. Money buys access to hitherto closed knowledge or roles. Even getting in touch with nature and the cycle of the year can be commodified. Gwydion McPagan's Moon Calendar keeps you abreast of the eight-fold calendar, as well as giving handy hints on when to cut your wand. There are special seasonal workshops and meditations, particular *Samhain, Imbolc, Beltane* or *Lughnasa* incense to be obtained from outlets like Starchild Apothecary, events such as Glastonbury's University of Avalon's Samhain Council of Wise Women weekend, or the Lammas Full Moon Celtic Camp.

To conclude, then, we are undoubtedly experiencing an upsurge of interest in and speculation about the Celts. For many Britons, the Noble Savages are back and they are unquestionably Celts. The marketing possibilities to which this trend gives rise are immense, and the general public is attracted to merchandise which is perceived to be Celtic. However, alongside and within the general market, there is a specialist clientele, for whom the commodification of the Celt is not simply commercial or aesthetic but spiritual. The worldviews and ethos of New

Age and Pagan religiosity open up a whole new area of consumerism, in which, as I trust I have demonstrated, ingenuity knows no bounds. Whether this aspect of the marketing of tradition is producing spiritual empowerment or simply Celtic kitsch is for the individual to decide.[4]

REFERENCES

Bowman, Marion. 1993. Reinventing the Celt. *Religion* 23:47–156.

Constantine, Pamela. 1993. Borderlands: The Celtic World of Imagination, and the Arts. *Celtic Connections* 5 (December):10.

Davis, Courtney. 1989. *Art of Celtia*. London: Blandford.

———. 1994. *Celtic Mandalas*. London: Blandford.

Gannon, Alban J. and Rosmary Feld. 1992. *Quest* 91 (September):20.

Heelas, Paul. 1992. The sacralization of the self and New Age capitalism. In *Social Change in Contemporary Britain*, ed. N. Abercrombie and A. Ward, pp. 139–166. Cambridge: Polity Press.

———. 1993. The New Age in Cultural Context: The Premodern, the Modern and the Postmodern. *Religion* 23:103–116.

James, David. 1993. *The Little Book of Celtic Designs*. Shaftesbury: Element Books.

Matthews, Caitlin. 1989. *Elements of Celtic Tradition*. Shaftesbury: Element Books.

———. 1993. *Celtic Book of the Dead*. London: St Martin's Press.

——— and John Matthews. 1993. *The Little Book of Celtic Wisdom*. Shaftesbury: Element Books.

Matthews, John. 1992. *Celtic Shamanism*. Shaftesbury: Element Books.

Raschke, Carl. 1992. Fire and roses, or the problem of postmodern religious thinking. In *Shadow of Spirit: Postmodernism and Religion*, ed. P. Berry and A. Wernick, p. 104. London: Routledge.

Spence, Louis. 1993. *Mysteries of Britain*. Studio Editions.

---

[4]My background is in Religious Studies and Folklore; I am interested in what people believe and how they act on those beliefs, the practice rather than the theory of religion. As this paper was written for a conference with the focus 'The Marketing of Tradition', it is the commercial aspect of New Age/Neo-pagan Celticism which is highlighted. This is not to play down the spiritual aspects and importance of what is happening, about which I have written elsewhere.

£12.95 3/4/96

Folklore in Use

Applications in the Real World

Volume 2 Number 1

1994

CONTENTS

ISBN 1 874312 21 4

Printed in Great Britain by Antony Rowe Ltd, Chippenham, Wiltshire

Contributors

Ann Berriman is a playwrite, producer and art critic from Sydney, Australia.

Marion Bowman is a Research Fellow at the Bath College of Higher Education in England.

Teri Brewer lectures at the University of Glamorgan in Wales.

Clodagh Harvey is a specialist in Irish oral narrative. She is Project Officer for the Historic Monuments and Buildings Branch, Department of the Environment in Northern Ireland.

Leslie Jones is an itinerant scholar of Celtic Studies and Folklore based in Eugene, Oregon, and a former Fulbright Scholar in Wales.

Gwendolyn Leick lectures at the University of Glamorgan in Wales.

Viv Loveday has almost two decades of involvement in re-enactment societies, and lectures at the University of Glamorgan

John Niles teaches in the Department of English at the University of California at Berkeley.

Josey Petford is a student at the University of Glamorgan.

John Sheets teaches anthropology at Central Missouri State University.

Gerald Thomas is Professor of Folklore at Memorial University in Newfoundland, Canada.

Patricia Atkinson Wells is a consultant folklorist working in the Business and Economic Research Center at Middle Tennessee State University.

Juliette Wood is an honorary lecturer in the Department of Welsh at the University of Wales in Cardiff.

Pauline Young is Course Leader in Women's Studies at the University of Glamorgan where she lectures in Literature, Theatre and Popular Culture.